MW00889971

MASTER YOUR SUCCESS

TIMELESS PRINCIPLES TO DEVELOP INNER
CONFIDENCE AND CREATE AUTHENTIC
SUCCESS

THIBAUT MEURISSE

Edited by
KERRY J DONOVAN

CONTENTS

Who is this book for   vii
Introduction   ix
How to use this book   xiii

SECTION I
TAKING RESPONSIBILITY

1. Start where you are   3
2. Take one hundred percent responsibility for your life   5
3. Take extra responsibility   7
4. Forget about luck   9
5. Value your time above all   12
6. Follow your own path   14
7. Embrace your destiny   16
8. Forgive yourself and others   18

SECTION II
KNOWING YOURSELF

9. Cultivate self-awareness   23
10. Define what success means to you   25
11. Know what you want   27
12. Know what matters to you   29
13. Know your strength   32
14. Embrace your weaknesses   35
15. Listen to your intuition   38

SECTION III
DECIDING WHO YOU WANT TO BE

16. Decide who you're going to be   43
17. Be intentional during your day   45
18. Raise your standards   48
19. Cultivate self-discipline   50
20. Build accountability   52
21. Create a morning ritual   54
22. Find people worth fighting for   57

SECTION IV
LIVING IN INTEGRITY

23. Respect yourself   61
24. Practice radical honesty with yourself   63
25. Practice radical honesty with others   65
26. Learn to say no   68
27. Set clear rules and boundaries   70
28. Show up on time   72
29. Take pride in your work   74
30. Cultivate a passion for what you do   76
31. Ask for what you want   79
32. Be a producer, not a consumer   82

SECTION V
CULTIVATING CONFIDENCE

33. Believe you can   87
34. Believe that who you are and what you do matters   89
35. Challenge your limiting beliefs   91
36. Focus on what you want   93
37. Cultivate optimism   96
38. Perceive the opportunities around you   98
39. Think big   101
40. Believe you will improve long-term   103
41. Celebrate your success   105
42. Move beyond your comfort zone   107
43. Practice positive self-talk   110
44. Practice visualization   113

SECTION VI
DEVELOPING AN ACCURATE MODEL OF REALITY

45. Understand that success is a process   117
46. Align yourself with reality   119
47. See failures as part of the process   121
48. Look for role models   123
49. Dramatically reduce your learning curve   125
50. Focus on solutions   127
51. Don't assume, verify   129
52. Cultivate long-term thinking   132
53. Schedule thinking time   134
54. Challenge the status quo   136

55. Ask smart questions   138

56. Take calculated risks   141

57. Better anticipate   144

SECTION VII
GETTING THINGS DONE

58. Set daily goals   149

59. Finish what you start   151

60. Think less, do more   153

61. Leverage The 80/20 Principle   155

62. Maximize your speed of implementation   158

63. Get started   160

64. Focus on the process   162

65. Think projects not tasks   164

66. Focus on one thing at a time   166

67. Eliminate distractions and boost your focus   168

68. Go temporarily out of balance   171

69. Be a master, not a dabbler   173

70. Fall in love with consistency   176

71. Take effective breaks   179

SECTION VIII
MAINTAINING AN OPEN MIND

72. Leverage your curiosity   185

73. Embrace flexibility   187

74. Never stop learning   189

75. Stay humble   191

76. Make the most of your mistakes   193

77. Let go of your ego   195

SECTION IX
DEVELOPING EMOTIONAL RESILIENCE

78. Embrace patience   199

79. Treat each day as a new beginning   201

80. Focus on what you can control   204

81. Leverage the power of reframing   207

82. Honor the struggle   209

83. Cultivate self-compassion   211

84. Prepare for the worst   213

85. Practice gratitude   215

86. Learn from your emotions   218

87. Exercise regularly   221

SECTION X

INFLUENCING AND INSPIRING OTHERS

88. Share your dreams/broadcast your desires   227

89. See yourself as a role model   230

90. Aim to change yourself before changing others   232

91. Add value to other people's lives   234

92. Believe in the potential of others   236

93. Be obsessed with your customers   238

94. Compliment others   240

95. Seek a win-win   242

96. Ask more questions, give fewer answers   244

97. Listen more, talk less   246

98. Put yourself in the shoes of other people   249

99. Surround yourself with successful people   252

100. Focus on building long-term relationships   254

Conclusion   257

What do you think?   259

Master Your Emotions (PREVIEW)   261

Other Books By The Authors: 271

About the Author   273

Action Guide   275

Do you want more success in your personal and professional life? Do you have big goals and dreams but are struggling to achieve them?

This book is for you if you:

- Know you're capable of more but don't know where to start,
- Have big goals and dreams but are unsure how to make them a reality,
- Feel out of alignment with your true self, and/or
- Want to become your best self and make a bigger impact on the world.

If any or all of the above points apply to you, read on.

INTRODUCTION

What if, by applying specific principles and ways of thinking, you could skyrocket your chances of achieving success in any area of your life?

Imagine if, by understanding a handful of key principles and adopting a couple of new daily habits, you could be in a completely different place, mentally, physically, financially and spiritually in just a few years from now?

Wouldn't that get you excited?

Many people assume they need to be lucky to be successful. They hope for the big breakthrough that will allow them to reach the level of success they most desire. If only they could obtain that promotion, get that celebrity endorsement for their book, or meet the right person, then they would finally "make it."

Here's the problem:

That major breakthrough you're waiting for might never happen.

What if I told you that you don't need any major breakthrough to move from where you are to where you want to be? The idea you could become successful overnight if that one event were to occur is largely a myth. For 99.99% of people (or more), this lucky break will never happen. Simply because reality doesn't work that way. Relying on this type of "black swan" event is not a strategy. Or, to put it differently, *luck is not a strategy*.

Now, it is true that luck will play a role in how successful you are in your endeavors and how fast you'll achieve your goals. However, as we'll discuss in detail in this book, success is *not* a single event. It's not something that happens overnight thanks to one lucky incident. Success is a process. It is the result of consistent hard work carried out strategically on a daily basis and sustained over a long period of time. What we called "luck" is often simply the result of sticking to a certain process for long enough.

Success is:

- The writer who finally sees decent sales after releasing his seventh book (that's me),
- The person who goes on dozens and dozens of dates and finally finds a suitable partner, and
- The aspiring coach who offers his or her services for free and continuously improves until he or she can finally make a living from coaching.

The point is, there are specific things that will dramatically increase your odds of success. In this book, we'll introduce one hundred actionable things to enhance your chances of success. I'm not a big believer in luck—and you shouldn't believe in luck either. There are much better strategies available than simply relying on luck. It is time to discover these strategies and put them into practice.

What you will discover in this book

This book is divided into ten sections and follows a logical order.

In **Section I**, *Taking responsibility*, you'll learn why it's critical to take responsibility for your life and your actions and how this will open tremendous opportunities for growth while increasing your chances of achieving your goals.

In **Section II**, *Knowing yourself*, you'll discover why developing self-awareness is so important and how to achieve it. We'll outline the importance of knowing your strengths and weaknesses, identifying your values, and describing your definitions of success.

In **Section III**, *Deciding who you want to be*, we'll discuss the importance of being fully committed to designing the life you desire. You'll be invited to raise your standards and create more accountability in your life.

In **Section IV**, *Living with integrity*, you'll learn why you must affirm your right to exist in this world and fully express yourself.

In **Section V**, *Cultivating confidence*, you'll be introduced to the incredible power of confidence. You'll discover why it is absolutely critical to develop rock-solid confidence and keep focusing on the countless opportunities around you.

In **Section VI**, *Developing an accurate model of reality*, you'll practice aligning yourself with reality. By understanding how reality works and by identifying the best course of action to achieve your goals, you'll dramatically enhance your chances of success.

In **Section VII**, *Getting things done*, you'll discover key principles that will allow you to boost your focus and massively improve your productivity. As a result, you'll obtain results significantly faster than you otherwise would.

In **Section VIII**, *Maintaining an open mind*, we'll see why it's important you stay open-minded. By developing an open mind, you'll be able to learn faster, gather information more effectively and make better decisions. This, in turn, will improve your results.

In **Section IX**, *Developing emotional resilience*, you'll discover one of the key secrets to success: the ability to maintain a positive state of mind even during challenging times. Being able to stay positive will allow you to keep going no matter what until you achieve your goals.

In the final section, **Section X**, *Influencing and Inspiring Others*, you'll learn how to work with others effectively. By being able to cooperate with others, inspire others and surround yourself with the right people, you'll improve your results exponentially.

As you apply the principles in each section diligently, you'll maximize your chances of achieving your most audacious goals and dreams.

It is essential to remember that success is a process, so don't expect it to happen overnight. However, if you keep working on yourself and moving toward your goals every day consistently, you'll be well on your way to achieving your most exciting goals.

Are you ready?

HOW TO USE THIS BOOK

I recommend you read this book all the way through once first. Then, I invite you to revisit it and complete the exercises at the end of each chapter. Each principle, when applied, will enhance the chances of you reaching your goals. So, make sure you familiarize yourself with each of them.

Don't hesitate to read this book as many times as necessary in the coming months or years. Repetition is the key to success.

Your Free Step-By-Step Action Guide

To help you master the success principles introduced in this book, I've created a free action guide. You can download it at the following URL:

https://whatispersonaldevelopment.org/master-your-success

If you have any difficulty downloading the action guide, contact me at:

thibaut.meurisse@gmail.com and I will send you a copy as soon as possible.

Alternatively, you can use the guide available at the end of this book.

SECTION I

TAKING RESPONSIBILITY

In the long run, we shape our lives, and we shape ourselves. The process never ends until we die. And the choices we make are ultimately our own responsibility.

— Eleanor Roosevelt, former First Lady of the United States.

You're responsible for your life. You cannot delegate your life to someone else or expect others to do the work for you. For things to change, you have to change. In this section, we'll review the key principles you can use to regain control over your life and become the creator of your own destiny.

Let's get started.

1

START WHERE YOU ARE

 You cannot escape the responsibility of tomorrow by evading it today.

— ABRAHAM LINCOLN, FORMER PRESIDENT OF THE
UNITED STATES.

Are you trying to escape your present reality? Do you wish you could be somewhere else?

Like many of us, you may believe you deserve more. You should be making more money, have better relationships or be healthier, right? There's nothing wrong with wanting the best for yourself and for the people around you. However, believing you should be somewhere else is arguing against the nature of reality, and reality can never be wrong. The truth is that *you are exactly where you're supposed to be at this point in time.*

Trying to be somewhere else creates tension, generates stress and can lead to disappointment or even depression. More importantly, it prevents you from looking at reality objectively.

Why does this matter? Because a major part of designing a successful life comes from your ability to develop an accurate model of reality. And to do this, you must first understand reality and accept it the way it is (see also *Section VI, Developing an Accurate Model of Reality*).

Your current situation is a fact. The question is: what are you going to do about it? Although you cannot change your past, you can always change your future by taking action in the present.

Remember, success is a process. It consists of key habits and tasks that, when performed consistently, move you closer to your goals. Furthermore, you can start the process right here, right now. In fact, this is the only thing you can do to improve your life.

You cannot attain success simply by marrying the ideal partner. You must nurture the relationship every day (i.e., focus on the process). Otherwise, your marriage will fall apart.

Nor can you achieve success just by hitting a specific revenue target with your business. You must put in place a process that will allow you to keep your business afloat for years to come. If you stop working on your business, sooner or later, you're likely to become bankrupt.

You're only truly successful when you do your best to reach worthy goals every day. And you can do this starting today, regardless of your current situation.

So, wherever you are right now is fine. Start here and now with what you have, and keep moving forward.

* * *

Action step

- Acknowledge that you are exactly where you're supposed to be *at this moment* and let go of any sense of pressure.
- Get excited about all the things you can do to improve and start moving toward your dreams.

2

TAKE ONE HUNDRED PERCENT RESPONSIBILITY FOR YOUR LIFE

 There is an expiry date on blaming your parents for steering you in the wrong direction; the moment you are old enough to take the wheel, responsibility lies with you.

— J.K. ROWLING, NOVELIST.

Are you taking one hundred percent responsibility for your life, or do you blame other people and general circumstances for your current situation?

The key to making your success inevitable is to take absolute responsibility for your life. This is the most powerful thing you can do to transform your life. You must take responsibility for all your actions and accept that you are mainly where you are right now, because of who you are and what you do.

If you want to be somewhere else, the way you think and the way you act will have to change. Your core beliefs will have to change. What you do every day will have to change. As you start thinking and acting differently, you cannot fail to alter the course of your destiny.

Taking responsibility is critical

People like to blame the actions of others or bad luck for their situation. Sometimes, at least to some extent, it is undeniable that an event or situation may have been caused by external factors. You may feel as though you've been wronged or that something bad that happened wasn't your fault.

Taking responsibility, however, has nothing to do with apportioning blame or being right. It doesn't matter who was right and who was wrong in the past. You're merely looking at what *you* can do to improve your current situation.

To end up where you want to be, you need to take one hundred percent responsibility for your life. As you do so, you will reclaim absolute control over your life, which will maximize your chance of achieving all your future goals and dreams.

* * *

Action step

Write down two or three things you would do differently if you were to take one hundred percent responsibility for everything in your life.

3

TAKE EXTRA RESPONSIBILITY

 The price of greatness is responsibility.

— Winston Churchill, politician, historian, and
artist.

Taking extra responsibility means that you are willing to accept as much responsibility as possible, taking on even more of the blame than you probably deserve.

For instance, let's imagine you delegate a task to someone, and they don't complete the job properly. Your first reaction might be to blame the person for their incompetence. Instead, you should ask yourself, "In what way am I responsible in this situation?" Perhaps you asked the wrong person to complete the task. Maybe you didn't give them the right instructions, or you may have failed to follow up and monitor the progress of the project. As you can see, even in this specific situation, you are actually responsible for the outcome of the task.

In fact, when you trace a problem back to its origins, you'll often find you could have avoided the issue if you had taken more care when delegating the task. Maybe you could have taken more time to plan, or you could have asked for advice, or maybe you could have been less complacent. To address this issue, I encourage you to work through the following exercise:

1. Look at one thing that currently bothers you.
2. Try to find the root cause.
3. Then, decide what you could have done differently to prevent the issue from happening in the first place.

By completing this exercise, you may realize how much overall responsibility you had for the outcome. One benefit of taking extra responsibility is that you will become better at anticipating problems. As you regularly ask yourself, "How am I responsible here," you will train your mind to look for ways to think and act differently. This, in turn, will help you prevent similar problems from happening in the future (e.g., asking the wrong person to do a task in the first place).

Take more responsibility for your life than anybody else and you'll see that, in the long run, your life will improve dramatically. The truth is that nothing in your life can change until you do. If you want your life to change, the change will have to start with you (see also *Chapter 57. Better Anticipate*).

Action step

Make sure you complete the exercise previously mentioned using your action guide. For reminder:

1. Select one thing that bothers you.
2. Find the root cause.
3. Decide what you could have done to prevent that issue from happening.

4

FORGET ABOUT LUCK

 Luck is the residue of design.

— HOWARD SCHULTZ, BUSINESSMAN.

Are you hoping to get lucky one day and finally achieve the success you want?

Many people see success as an event, something that will happen one day if they are lucky enough. This is the myth of overnight success.

However, in truth, success is a process. Success is the result of consistent hard work done (almost) daily over a long period of time. Sure, luck can help you achieve your goals faster, but in the long term, luck is mostly irrelevant.

A writer can write ten books and still not see any significant results in terms of copies sold or money generated from the sales. However, if he or she keep writing more books and never stops learning about the industry, he or she will likely achieve decent results over the long term. That's more or less what happened to me.

Similarly, it may require more time than you initially expected, but if you persevere and do things the right way, you will most likely achieve your goals in the long run. The key to success is to develop an accurate model of reality while continuously learning from setbacks and failures.

Now, why is believing in luck such a big issue? Because the very moment you begin to rely on luck, you give your power away to external circumstances. By doing so, you rob yourself of your true potential and significantly reduce your chances of attaining your goals.

In short, believing in luck is the opposite of taking personal responsibility.

You can either rely on luck, or you can take one hundred percent responsibility and do *absolutely everything in your power* to obtain the results you desire.

A bit of luck can certainly help, but it's not the major component that will determine whether you succeed or fail. Identifying the best course of action, designing the most effective process and sticking to it consistently, will.

Therefore, forget about luck. Stop hoping or wishing for good fortune. Instead, identify the most effective way to move from where you are now to where you want to be. Then, put in place the right process by setting clear goals and creating daily routines. Finally, stick to the process.

In the section *VI. Developing an accurate model of reality* and *VII. Getting things done*, we'll see in more detail how to create an effective process that will maximize the odds you'll achieve your goals.

Action step

Write down the answer to the following question in your action guide:

If luck didn't exist, what would I do to maximize my chances of achieving my biggest goal?

5

VALUE YOUR TIME ABOVE ALL

 Until we can manage time, we can manage nothing else.

— Peter F. Drucker, management consultant.

How much would I need to pay you to get an hour of your time? $10? $25? $100? $1,000?

Time is one of the scarcest resources on earth. Thus, it's your responsibility to use your time well. As you learn to use your time wisely, you cannot fail to skyrocket your productivity, increase your wealth and free more time to do the things you really love.

The major difference between successful people and others is in the value they give to their time. Successful people manage their time ruthlessly. They go the extra mile to ensure they make effective use of it and continually try to protect it or save more of it.

For instance, successful people:

- **Hire coaches, seek mentors or buy courses** to learn what they need as quickly as possible (i.e., they never try to reinvent the wheel).

- **Set crystal clear goals and identify priorities** to ensure they spend most of their time working on key tasks.
- **Act with a sense of urgency** by setting specific deadlines to force them to get things done, and
- **Say no to (almost) everything** that isn't in line with their vision or values.

On the other hand, unsuccessful people behave as though they'll live forever. They mistakenly believe that time is abundant, that they will never run out of it. As a result, they procrastinate, waste time on unproductive tasks or spend hours glued to the TV. Why bother doing anything important today? There will always be tomorrow, right?

Understand that each day, you have a choice. You can use your time well to create the life you want, or you can waste it by pursuing trivial things. But remember, each second that passes is gone. Forever.

Don't assume your future self will be more productive or any wiser than your present self. It most likely won't. After all, your future self is the product of what your present self does today. So, start using your time well *today* because, if you don't, chances are you won't tomorrow either (see also *Section VII, Getting Things Done*).

Action step

Using your action guide, answer the following questions:

- What exactly does "valuing your time" mean to me?
- What are two specific things I could do to make better use of my time?

FOLLOW YOUR OWN PATH

 Be yourself; everyone else is already taken.

— OSCAR WILDE, WRITER.

What would you do if nobody expected anything from you? Would you still be doing the same things every day, or would you do things differently?

In life, you have two choices:

1. Follow your own path and express your unique personality, or
2. Act like most people and pretend to be someone you're not in the hope of being accepted.

We love relying on experts to guide us and tell us how to live our lives. However, the truth is, no one can give us the answers we need to live life on our own terms.

No expert or guru can live your life for you. No person can eat your food, take care of your health or think your thoughts. Nobody can make your decisions for you.

Consequently, to succeed on your own terms you must be willing to trust yourself and become a truly independent thinker. You must get rid of the thoughts and ideas that do not belong to you. You must abandon the goals and dreams that aren't yours. Then, you must summon the courage to act in line with your values—not the values other people seek to impose on you.

Perhaps an interesting way to see your life is as a journey through which you affirm your character and build your strengths so that you can accomplish your destiny (not someone else's).

How often do you do things because it's what everybody else does? If you were being absolutely honest with yourself, what specific things would you start or stop doing?

People we admire are often those who are true to themselves. This is probably because they tell us who we could be if we decided to follow our own path.

So, what does your unique path look like? What would the successful and happy version of you do?

* * *

Action step

Using your action guide, answer the following questions:

- If I were to follow my own path, what would I be doing?
- If I didn't have to worry about what my family, friends, colleagues or society think, what would I be doing?

EMBRACE YOUR DESTINY

 It is not in the stars to hold our destiny, but in ourselves.

— William Shakespeare, dramatist and playwright.

Are you running away from your true calling?

It's easier to play it safe than it is to face your fears and move toward your loftiest aspirations, but for how long will you keep running away from those fears? Realize that your deepest fears often indicate what you *should* be doing. They're telling you which direction to go. They're inviting you to grow and become more than you are.

Sure, you can decide to stay within your comfort zone. One problem though—nothing ever grows there! Therefore, sooner or later, you have a choice to make. You can embrace your destiny or reject it, you can make yourself bigger by facing your fears, or you can shrink by running away from them.

Every time you confront your fears, you expand your comfort zone. As you do so, you open yourself up to new possibilities. There is no telling what you can do once you start facing your fears and chasing ambitious goals. Most people greatly underestimate what they're capable of achieving in the long term. They fail to realize how much more they can become if they develop more courage over time.

Do you imagine what you could accomplish in ten years if you took the first step toward your dreams today?

For now, you don't need to know *how* your vision will play out. You merely need to acknowledge your destiny, accept it and take the first step in the right direction. Eventually, what you have to do will be revealed to you. As a result, over time, you'll be able to refine your vision and gain clarity (see also, *Chapter 63. Get started*).

Action step

Answer the following questions:

- What is my true calling? What's my intuition telling me?
- What fears do I need to overcome to move in the right direction?

FORGIVE YOURSELF AND OTHERS

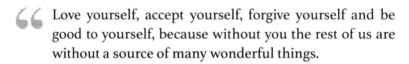 Love yourself, accept yourself, forgive yourself and be
good to yourself, because without you the rest of us are
without a source of many wonderful things.

— LEO F. BUSCAGLIA, AUTHOR AND MOTIVATIONAL
SPEAKER.

Do you blame yourself for past mistakes? Do you resent others for
what they did to you years ago?

You cannot move forward if you keep carrying the burden of the past.
The truth is, your past is long gone. It doesn't exist anymore. The
only thing that exists is your memory of it. In fact, the story you tell
yourself keeps you a prisoner of the past.

Fortunately, there is no rule saying you must keep the same old story
forever. At any time, you have the ability to make different decisions
that will alter the future course of your life. This means you can
change your past by thinking different thoughts in the present. In
fact, this is the only thing you can do.

So, forgive yourself for all your past mistakes. Then, focus on what you can do *now* to design a better future. In the past, you did the best you could, based on what you knew at the time. It's now time to move on.

In the same way, forgive others. Not because you're a nice person, but because you value your well-being and happiness above anything else. Also, understand that what people did to you has less to do with you and more to do with them and their issues.

In conclusion, release the weight of the past. Instead, use it as a lesson to build your future—starting today! As the saying goes, "Resentment is like drinking poison and then waiting for the other person to die." Resenting other people or hating yourself for something you did or didn't do in the past is of no use. Hating others won't make things any better. And hating yourself won't help either.

So, forgive yourself, forgive others and start stepping into your ideal future. Let go of who you were to become who you want to be (see also *Chapter 83 Cultivate Self-Compassion*).

Action step

Take a couple of minutes to:

- Acknowledge that your peace of mind is more important than anything anyone may have done to you in the past. Stop trying to be right, try to be happy.
- Forgive yourself for mistakes you may have made in the past. You did what you could based on what you knew and who you were at the time.

SECTION II

KNOWING YOURSELF

No one man can, for any considerable time, wear one face to himself, and another to the multitude, without finally getting bewildered as to which is the true one.

— NATHANIEL HAWTHORNE, NOVELIST.

As the ancient Greek philosopher, Socrates, said, "*The unexamined life is not worth living*". In fact, it's almost impossible to design your ideal life if you don't know who you are and what you value the most. Some people spend years pursuing goals that aren't theirs. They live their lives based on what society tells them they should be doing. And when they reach the end of their lives, they realized they have been lying to themselves.

In this section, we'll cover some key principles that will help you discover who you really are and what you really want from life. The more self-awareness you cultivate, the more you'll be able to design a life that suits you—and the more fulfilled you'll be.

Let's get started.

9

CULTIVATE SELF-AWARENESS

 Awareness is the greatest agent for change.

— ECKHART TOLLE, SPIRITUAL TEACHER.

Self-awareness is the ability to learn about yourself every day and your ability to self-reflect. It is the mechanism through which you give yourself feedback to help you grow as a conscious human being. Thus, it is a powerful catalyst for growth. The more self-aware you are, the more opportunities you have to improve and become all you can be.

Most successful people are highly self-aware. They continuously work on understanding who they are and what they really want from life. In addition, they keep refining their vision and look for blind spots and other biases they may fall victim to. Self-awareness brings them more clarity, and clarity is power. The more we know ourselves, the happier and more successful we'll tend to be.

The truth is, you repeatedly fall prey to various biases and become unable to look at yourself objectively. Due to the complexity of the world and the way your brain works, your thinking is bound to be highly inaccurate. Hence, the need for more self-awareness in your life.

Here is what being self-aware entails (among other things):

- Knowing your strengths and weaknesses,
- Knowing what really matters to you (and what doesn't),
- Acknowledging your feelings instead of suppressing them,
- Identifying your disempowering thought patterns,
- Living in the present moment as much as you can (instead of being lost in your thoughts), and
- Uncovering your blind spots and biases.

To develop more self-awareness:

- Never stop learning about yourself,
- Let go of external pressure and look within,
- Become an observer of your thoughts, feelings and actions, and
- Try to understand who you are and what you really want.

Action step

Using your action guide, answer the following questions:

- If I were to be more self-aware, what specific thing would have the biggest positive impact on my life?
- What is the one negative emotion I experience most often?
- What is the underlying belief causing me to feel this way?

DEFINE WHAT SUCCESS MEANS TO YOU

 Always be yourself, express yourself, have faith in yourself, do not go out and look for a successful personality and duplicate it.

— BRUCE LEE, ACTOR AND MARTIAL ARTIST.

Have you ever taken the time to define exactly what success means to you?

We all want to be successful, but we often fail to define what success means to us. We let society decide what we should value and, as a result, can spend our entire life chasing the wrong goals.

Perhaps you're obsessed with climbing the corporate ladder. Perhaps you want to buy a spacious house in a nice neighborhood. Perhaps you want to keep up with the Joneses and fit in.

Although there is nothing wrong with any of these aspirations, they don't necessarily guarantee a happy life. You may be stuck in an unfulfilling career because you chose a job that gives you high social status, or you may try too hard to keep up with the Joneses while you'd be better off changing neighborhoods to be around like-minded people.

There is no one definition of success.

Only you can decide what success should look like. However, to do this, you must stop seeking other people's approval and be honest enough with yourself to accept the notion that your current situation is not what *you* want. You must give yourself total permission to rethink your life and follow your own path. This might entail making difficult decisions, such as quitting your job, ending a relationship, or cutting people out of your life.

But, remember that if you don't clarify what success means to you, you risk living your life according to someone else's definition of success. And, this particular definition is unlikely to bring you the fulfillment you seek.

The bottom line is, you are responsible for your success, and it starts by deciding exactly what success means to you. So, if you could live your life the way you want, what would it look like? What would you be doing? Who would you be around? What would your ideal day be like?

* * *

Action step

Using your action guide, write down five must-haves for a successful life. Then, based on these must-haves, try to come up with your own personal definition of success and summarize it in one or two sentences.

11

KNOW WHAT YOU WANT

 Know what you want. Clarity is power. And vague goals promote vague results.

— ROBIN SHARMA, AUTHOR AND MOTIVATIONAL SPEAKER.

Your energy is limited, and the world around you competes to get a piece of it. If you don't know what you want, you risk spending your life (and energy) working for someone who does know what he or she wants. To avoid this, you *must* make the most of your energy by turning it into a superpower. How? Through clarity and focus.

Energy only gains power when it is directed toward a specific thing. For instance, it is by channeling sun rays that a magnifying glass can start a fire, which is why clarity is key. Clarity enables focus. Once you know what you want, you can direct all your energy toward a focal point. Instead of scattering your energy, you will be using it effectively. This laser-like focus on a specific goal will produce extraordinary results in the long term.

Also, knowing what you want tells your subconscious what to look for. It will then work for you 24/7. As a result, you'll find yourself coming up with ideas during your sleep, while brushing your teeth or while travelling to work. You'll encounter new opportunities and may even notice strange coincidences.

Finally, it's only by knowing what you want that you can create a crystal-clear plan to move from where you are to where you want to be.

The point is, clarity is power.

Most successful people know what they want. Ask them what they're working on and they'll tell you their goals in great detail. Not only that, but they'll also tell you exactly how they plan to achieve them.

What about you? Can you tell people your goals without even having to think about it? If not, write down exactly what you want. The more clarity you have, the better.

Remember, clarity leads to extraordinary results, while vagueness leads to mediocrity. Again, if you lack clarity, you'll often end up working for someone else who knows exactly what he or she wants (see also *Chapter 58. Set daily goals*).

* * *

Action step

Spend five to ten minutes brainstorming answers to the question, "What do I really want?"

Do this for each area of your life: career, finance, health, personal growth relationships and spirituality.

12

KNOW WHAT MATTERS TO YOU

 Your core values are the deeply held beliefs that authentically describe your soul.

— JOHN C. MAXWELL, AUTHOR, SPEAKER AND PASTOR.

Do you know what matters the most to you? And, if you do, are you living by these core values?

In your daily life, you continuously have to make decisions. Your ability to make one sound decision after another will dramatically impact the direction your life takes. Now, how can you simplify your decision-making process and ensure you make life-enhancing decisions?

Well, you need specific criteria on which to base your decisions. This is when values come in handy. Values act as an effective framework for decision-making. They allow you to eliminate any incongruent options, and they will help you make better decisions and make them more quickly.

For example, let's say you value autonomy above anything else. If so, when having to choose between a regular 9-5 job and being self-employed, you'll probably choose the latter. However, if you're unsure of your core values, making the right decision won't be as straightforward.

In short, by knowing your values, you can focus your energy and time on things that enhance your life. This is why identifying your core values and living by them is critical to living a life of integrity. Also, without clear values, you can become easily influenced by your environment, and this can lead you to make poor decisions. Thus, to reclaim power over your life, you need to clarify your values. Then, make these core values the rock-solid pillars on which you can base most of your decisions.

Now, here are two key characteristics to look for when it comes to your values:

1. **You must live by them.** Values are something you live by. They are part of you and seem right to you. They are *not* things you believe you should do because your parents or society say so.

2. **They must be specific.** Values aren't generic, rather they are personal. For instance, it is not enough to say that you value freedom. You must be able to articulate what freedom means to you. Is it being self-employed? Is it being debt-free? Is it owning only a few things? Or is it all of these and more?

The main takeaway is that, your core values create a framework for decision-making, allowing you to make better decisions and make them faster. They help you do the things that seem right to you and make you feel better about yourself.

So, spend time to identify your values and strive to live by them every day.

* * *

Action step

Complete the exercises below using your action guide:

- Write down your top ten values. If you're unsure what a value is, simply ask yourself what thing or concept you value the most (freedom, family, contribution, honesty et cetera).
- Select your top three values by asking yourself, "If I could choose only one value, what would it be?" Repeat the process until you have three values.
- On a scale of 1 to 10, where 1 is low and 10 is high, ask yourself how well you're living by these values.
- Finally, ask yourself, "Which is the one specific thing I could start doing today that will be more aligned with one or more of these values?"

13

KNOW YOUR STRENGTH

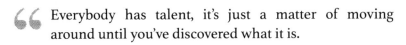 Everybody has talent, it's just a matter of moving
around until you've discovered what it is.

— GEORGE LUCAS, FILMMAKER.

What is (are) your superpower(s)? What is it that only you can do?

Knowing your talents and strengths is essential if you want to live a fulfilling life and realize your full potential. People who fail to do so may spend their entire life in a job they hate, feeling incompetent and of little use to society. If your working life is a constant struggle, and you feel as though every second at work is hell, you're probably not acting from your strengths.

Identify your strengths

Below are a few tips to help you identify your strengths:

1. **Ask people around you.** An effective way to find out what you're great at is to ask your family, friends, or colleagues.
2. **Look at what you do in your spare time.** What tasks do you volunteer for at work? What do you naturally do when left

alone? And what does this say about your potential strengths?

3. **Identify what you find easy to do, while other people find the same thing difficult.** Have you ever found yourself wondering why others can't do basic things such as *insert your answer here*? If so, that's a sign you've identified one of your strengths.

4. **Pay attention to what people compliment you for.** What do people around you say you're good at? Start noticing the compliments you receive. What does this say about your strengths?

5. **Lean toward what you enjoy doing.** Uncovering your strengths might take time. To begin the process, start by doing more of the things you enjoy or are curious about. Just lean in and see where it takes you.

Finally, when looking for your strengths, don't dismiss anything. A couple of seemingly "insignificant" strengths can make a major difference in your life. For instance, your strength could be your ability to:

-   Summarize information,
-   Organize events,
-   Make people feel at ease,
-   Study for hours, or
-   Care about people.

Double down on your strengths

Your time is limited. Therefore, rather than trying to overcome your weaknesses, focus on maximizing your strengths. Otherwise, you'll find yourself competing with people who are naturally gifted at what you struggle to do. There are exceptions though. If your weaknesses act as bottlenecks that prevent you from achieving your dreams, you might need to work on them first.

To sum up, identify your strengths and double down on them until you become outstanding. Then, see how things change for you.

Action step

Using your action guide, identify your biggest strengths by:

- Asking people around you,
- Looking at what you do during your spare time,
- Identifying what you can do easily (but others can't),
- Paying close attention to what people compliment you for, and
- Leaning toward what you enjoy doing.

14

EMBRACE YOUR WEAKNESSES

 My attitude is that if you push me towards something that you think is a weakness, then I will turn that perceived weakness into a strength.

— MICHAEL JORDAN, FORMER PROFESSIONAL BASKETBALL PLAYER.

Do you often beat yourself up?

Well, you have so many shortcomings, so it makes sense to do this, right? Guess what? So do the most successful people you look up to. However, rather than dwelling on their weaknesses and feeling sorry for themselves, successful people:

- Accept their weaknesses,
- Turn their weaknesses into strengths, and
- Ask for help when needed.

Accepting your weaknesses

The most successful people on this planet don't let their weaknesses or shortcomings determine what they can and cannot accomplish.

Instead, they acknowledge their weaknesses and accept them completely. Then, they focus on their strengths until they become outstanding at the few things they do well. In addition, they also attempt to turn their so-called weaknesses into strengths.

Turning "weaknesses" into strengths

Have you ever considered the notion that your "weaknesses" could actually be your biggest strengths?

In my personal life, I found that many of my weaknesses could actually be turned into powerful strengths, once I choose to embrace them.

For instance, I used to believe I was a little obsessive. But when I decided to take that obsession to the next level and become absolutely obsessed with one thing, things started changing for me. My business took off and I was able to move closer to my ideal life.

I also believed that, perhaps, I was too nice. But then I thought, what would happen if I decide to be the nicest person I can be and strive to help as many people as possible? By doing my best to remain a nice person and stay true to myself, I was able to help people in an authentic way while building connections with wonderful people in my industry. N.B. this example doesn't mean I'm saying yes to everyone and being a doormat.

I invite you to look at one of your weaknesses and ask yourself, "What would happen if I took that weakness to extreme lengths?"

If you're unsure what weaknesses you should focus on, try the following:

Identify "weaknesses" that seem to be unique to you and not shared by anybody else around you.

Your so-called weaknesses are often part of your personality. So, instead of changing who you are, think of ways you could turn your "weaknesses" into powerful strengths.

Asking for help

In the highly competitive world we're living in, if you try to do everything by yourself, you're likely to end up in trouble. Let's say you aren't good at math. How will you compete with people who excel at it?

This is why you need help. You must delegate or outsource work others can do better and/or faster than you. Some people out there will love doing the things you hate. These people could be accountants, writers or marketers.

Remember, doing everything by yourself will never allow you to become world-class at anything. If you truly want to excel, delegate all the things you do poorly and become obsessed over what you're already skilled at.

To sum up, never let your apparent shortcomings prevent you from achieving your goals. Embrace your perceived weaknesses, turn some of them into your biggest strengths and ask for help whenever you need it.

* * *

Action step

Write down what you believe to be your biggest weaknesses. Then ask yourself:

- What would happen if I took these weaknesses to extremes? How could I turn some of them into strengths?
- Who or what can help me overcome these weaknesses?

15

LISTEN TO YOUR INTUITION

 Intuition is really a sudden immersion of the soul into the universal current of life.

— Paulo Coelho, novelist.

Do you listen to your gut, or do you keep doing anything *except* what you feel you should be doing?

The last thing you should do is to live the life others want you to live. This would mean ignoring your own desires and vision, and failing to express yourself in an authentic way.

However, listening to your intuition can be hard. This is because most, if not all, your choices have been influenced by people around you. Your parents may have told you what career to pursue. Your friends may have nudged you to adopt a certain lifestyle. Or your colleagues may have encouraged you to be happy with the status quo.

So, specifically, what can you do to listen to your intuition and start doing what feels right to *you*?

1. Embrace silence

The first thing you can do is to silence external noises. Some of the things you can do are:

Spend time alone. Spend time on your own on a regular basis. You could decide to go on a mini retreat. Or you could do a digital detox and stay away from digital devices for 24 hours or even an entire week.

Sit in silence. Spend a few minutes in silence before going to bed and/or upon waking in the morning. Then, ask questions to your subconscious, your higher self or however you want to describe it. Some examples are:

- What do I really want?
- What would I do if I didn't have to meet the expectations of people around me?
- What would I do if I didn't try to impress anybody?
- What would I do if I could start my life all over again?

2. Learn to trust your intuition

The second thing you want to do is to practice trusting your intuition. To do so:

Start small. Start by making small inconsequential decisions based on your gut. Don't want to go to a party? Don't go. See someone as untrustworthy? Don't trust him or her. Feel like going somewhere? Go. By continuously listening to yourself, you will become better at trusting your intuition.

Listen to your emotions. If something makes perfect sense rationally speaking, but doesn't feel right, then perhaps you shouldn't do it. Maybe you shouldn't take that job, get into that relationship or move to that city. This is where you must be radically honest with yourself.

Trust your higher self and your loftiest vision. Let go of any self-imposed limitations. Imagine that your craziest goals are possible. Believe that you wouldn't have any goals or dreams unless they were achievable. Then, trust yourself and take the action that feels right to you.

Learn to listen to your intuition, because this is the only way to live the life that *you* want.

* * *

Action step

What single thing could you do to listen to your intuition better?

SECTION III

DECIDING WHO YOU WANT TO BE

The only person you are destined to become is the person you decide to be.

— RALPH WALDO EMERSON, ESSAYIST AND PHILOSOPHER.

If you don't broadcast to the world who you want to be and what you want to achieve, none of your dreams will become a reality. At some point, you must make a decision. You must decide who you are going to be. Then, every day, you must commit to becoming that person.

So, decide who you want to be and act like the person you want to be *every day*. In this section, we'll go over key principles that will help you do just that.

Shall we get started?

16

DECIDE WHO YOU'RE GOING TO BE

 Make a choice. Just decide what it's gonna be, who you're gonna be, how you are going to do it. Just decide. And from that point, the universe will get out of your way.

— WILL SMITH, ACTOR.

Are you *committed* to changing your life or are you merely interested?

If you're merely interested, sooner or later, you'll find an excuse to give up. However, if you're truly *committed,* you'll find a way to make your vision a reality.

Have you ever heard of people achieving extraordinary feats just by kind of wanting something?

No.

The people who achieve extraordinary feats have a burning desire, and they are one hundred percent committed to achieving whatever they set their eyes on.

Commitment is what activates your hidden talents and strengths, and transforms mediocrity into excellence. Thus, to become the person you want to be, you must decide who you're going to be and how you're going to achieve it. You must not let chance decide what your future is going to be. As the high-performance coach, Brendon Burchard, wrote, "*If you leave your growth to randomness, you'll always live in the land of mediocrity.*"

Most people daydream about a better future. They hope or wish that one day, maybe, they will achieve their goals—but they have no intention to do the actual work to reach them (and, deep down, they know it).

Successful people don't daydream—they visualize. They envision what they want with clear intent and absolute determination. They understand that what they keep thinking about with conviction will, in the long term, most likely become their reality. As a result, they continually project themselves into the future, behaving as if they were already there—and in their mind, they actually are.

To sum up, average people daydream. Successful people visualize. Average people have dreams. Successful people have goals.

What about you? On which side of the divide are you? Learn to activate the power of commitment and everything will start changing for you.

Just decide!

* * *

Action step

Look at one of your major goals. What would happen if you were absolutely committed to achieving it? What would you do if attaining this goal was a matter of life or death? Write down your answer in your action guide.

17

BE INTENTIONAL DURING YOUR DAY

 I think it is possible for ordinary people to choose to be extraordinary.

— ELON MUSK, FOUNDER OF TESLA INC. AND SPACEX.

Are you living with intention, having proactively decided how you want your day to unfold, or are you living by default, merely reacting to your environment?

Most people spend the majority of their time on autopilot, only being purposeful with their actions in rare moments of lucidity during the day. Instead of taking control of the day, these individuals let their external environment dictate their attitude.

It starts first thing in the morning when they hit the snooze button. With this simple act they already broadcast to the world they have no serious business to do and no exciting things to work on. Then, they start watching the breakfast news, letting negativity penetrate their mind.

You must understand this: *your intent is your superpower*. Intent is awareness in action. It is being conscious enough in the present to choose the best course of action to achieve your desired outcome in the future. Intent enables you to channel energy into the pursuit of meaningful endeavors. When you fail to live with intent, you leak energy all day long. This behavior will not allow you to achieve anything significant.

The lesson here is that *you'll never achieve extraordinary things until you use the power of intent and focus your energy on the things that matter the most to you.*

Now, what does living with intent actually mean? It means deciding how you want to feel and what action you're going to take—and, most importantly, why.

For instance, intent is deciding:

- How you want to feel when you wake in the morning —and why,
- What you want your attitude to be at work—and why,
- How you want to behave with your family when you return home from work—and why, and
- What tasks to work on—and why.

As a rule of thumb, the more intentional you are during your day, the more control you regain and retain over your life. As you practice setting daily intent, you will dramatically alter your life and be able to achieve most or all of your goals in the long term.

Therefore, start thinking of the best way to go about your day. Why do you wake up in the morning? At work, what is your intent? In a meeting, how do you want to be perceived? What does "spending quality time with your family" actually mean?

Set intents during your day and watch your productivity skyrocket and your happiness improve. Fail to do so and you'll merely exist by default.

The choice is yours.

Action step

Using your action guide, answer the following question:

What would it mean to me to have more "intent" during my day? What specific things would I do?

18

RAISE YOUR STANDARDS

 If you want to change your life you have to raise your standards.

— TONY ROBBINS, AUTHOR AND LIFE COACH.

Like any other human being, you were given the dignity of choice. You can choose to remain as you are, or you can decide today to raise your standards and expect more of yourself.

Often, the thing that differentiates two people isn't their IQ, it's the level at which they decided to play the game called "life". When you choose to see yourself as a high performer, you start feeling, thinking and acting differently. You stop tolerating toxic habits. You surround yourself with uplifting people. You set higher goals. You learn as much as you can and, as a result, you perform at a higher level.

The main idea is, you must learn to see yourself for who you can become, not for who you are now—or for who your family or friends *think* you are. The truth is, nobody will ever be able to see what *you* see. Consequently, the moment will come when you'll have to stand up for yourself and decide to believe in yourself more than anybody else ever will.

Realize that it doesn't matter what image of yourself you hold now, because you can always change that self-image. You can always be more and do more. What people around you think you can or cannot do is irrelevant; it's their business, not yours. Your job is to commit to raising your standards and, as you do so, you'll start to uncover your true potential.

What it means to raise one's standards

Among other things, raising your standards means:

- Deciding who you want to be—and not letting anyone tell you what is and isn't possible for you,
- Establishing key rules and habits in line with your new standards (e.g., it could be delivering on your promises every single time or implementing an empowering morning routine),
- Surrounding yourself with people who try to improve themselves and perform at their best, and
- Continually working on your personal growth and expecting yourself to become better every day.

So, today, you need to demand more of yourself and see how things change for you. Remember, nobody can ever prevent you from raising your standards—but you.

To learn simple strategies to raise your standards, you can also refer to my book *Upgrade Yourself: Simple Strategies to Transform Your Mindset, Improve Your Habits and Change Your Life*

Action step

If you chose to do one single thing to help you raise your standards significantly, what would it be?

19

CULTIVATE SELF-DISCIPLINE

 We do today what they won't, so tomorrow we can accomplish what they can't.

— DWAYNE JOHNSON, ACTOR AND PROFESSIONAL
WRESTLER.

Do you hate discipline? Do you wish you could do whatever you want whenever you want?

Then the first thing you must understand is that freedom can only exist within a structured environment. *Without rules, there is no freedom.*

Think of some of the great painters in history, such as Picasso. Picasso didn't invent cubism out of thin air. First, he spent years mastering the fundamentals of painting. Only then, after learning the rules, was he able to emancipate himself and begin innovating.

In the same way, freedom exists only within a structure. Only your ability to create solid structures in your life—daily habits and specific schedules—gives you freedom.

Without self-discipline, you might end up overweight, stuck in a job you hate, or unable to find enjoyment in life. Therefore, self-discipline is not optional. Sooner or later, you will pay the price for its lack. I like to say that if you can't discipline yourself, someone else will (such as your boss, if you're an employee). Think of it this way: if you have no control over your thoughts, emotions and actions, how much freedom do you really have?

For instance, if you lack self-discipline, you risk:

- Doing subpar work (and becoming stuck at a dead-end job),
- Having poor health (and lacking the energy to achieve all your dreams and goals), and
- Feeling dissatisfied with your life in general.

The main takeaway is, your ability to do what you should do, when you should do it, whether you feel like it or not, is what ultimately creates freedom. It's what enables you to make more money, retire early, make a living doing what you love, or create anything else you want in your life.

On a side note, having the absolute freedom to do anything you want, whenever you want, does not guarantee happiness. We are all creatures of habit. Without habits or schedules of some sort, we often end up feeling miserable.

In short, discipline is the price of freedom. Learn to discipline yourself and you'll be able to have anything you want in the long term.

* * *

Action step

To build self-discipline, choose one positive habit that would improve your life and resolve to stick to it for the next thirty days. Make sure you start small to avoid putting too much pressure on yourself.

20

BUILD ACCOUNTABILITY

 Accountability breeds response-ability.

— STEPHEN R. COVEY, AUTHOR, EDUCATOR AND
BUSINESSMAN.

Who will call you out if you don't follow through on your commitment?

Greatness requires that you not only demand more of yourself, but that you also ask others to hold you accountable.

How many projects would be abandoned halfway through without hard deadlines? How many books would be left unfinished without publishers pushing writers to complete their books? How many school essays would never be written if there were no external threats such as receiving an "F"? Most of the things in this world wouldn't be completed without deadlines and expectations from external parties.

Human beings always seem to have valid excuses not to get things done, whether it is due to perfectionism, lack of motivation or laziness. This is why successful people implement accountability systems to ensure they complete the task at hand. They hire coaches, work with accountability partners and set clear deadlines. They don't rely on temporary bursts of inspiration. Instead, they expect themselves to complete their tasks on time. Rather than waiting for motivation to kick in, they generate it through daily actions and specific routines.

You, too, must strive to complete the tasks or projects you start—and within a set deadline. By doing so, you'll see your productivity skyrocket and your results improve massively. It's better to work on very few projects and complete them one hundred percent, than to have multiple projects on your plate and never finish any of them.

In short, creating an accountability system allows you to regain control over your life by deciding what to work on and within what timeframe. Think about it this way. Would you rather set your own deadlines or have someone else telling you what to do and by when? Which option is more empowering?

Remember, if you don't choose to discipline yourself, someone else will, and this will prove far more constraining. So, what accountability system could you put in place to stay on track with your goals?

For more, see *Master Your Focus: A Practical Guide to Stop Chasing the Next Thing and Focus on What Matters Until It's Done.*

Action step

How could you build an accountability system that works for you?

Using your action guide, write down what your ideal accountability system would look like.

21

CREATE A MORNING RITUAL

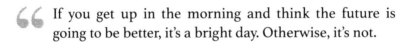 If you get up in the morning and think the future is going to be better, it's a bright day. Otherwise, it's not.

— Elon Musk, founder of Tesla Inc. and SpaceX.

What's the first thing you do when you wake up? Do you rely on specific habits to ensure you have a pleasant day, or do you let your environment dictate your mood?

Most people are reactive. They hit the snooze button in the morning and let everything affect their mood, from the bad weather to the negative news they read online. They fail to realize this simple truth: it's up to them to decide how they want to feel upon waking up. They can choose to be grateful, determined, or excited. They can envision their ideal day and take action accordingly.

Successful people seize the day. Successful people understand they must decide how they want to feel every day. To do so, they implement powerful daily habits. For instance, rather than checking their phone or turning on TV first thing in the morning, they take control of their emotional state whether by meditating, praying, expressing gratitude, or visualizing their goals. In addition, successful individuals plan their day to ensure they work on important tasks that move them closer to their goals.

There are two main reasons why morning rituals are so powerful:

1. **They allow you to take control of your mood.** As you stick to your morning ritual long term, you will automatically start feeling better the moment you wake up.
2. **They give you the opportunity to work on your key task(s) consistently.** As you focus on your most important task(s) first thing in the morning, you build momentum and skyrocket your productivity.

Below are three simple steps to create a powerful morning ritual:

1. **Decide what you want to get out of your morning ritual.** Choose how you want to feel and what actions you want to take. For instance, you may want to feel more grateful or more relaxed. Your specific actions may be to meditate or write down a few things you're grateful for.
2. **Start small to remove any friction.** For instance, meditate for a couple of minutes, write down three things you're grateful for or set one or two small daily goals.
3. **Stick to your morning ritual for at least thirty days.** Be consistent. This is key when it comes to implementing new habits and building momentum long term. Challenge yourself to stick to your morning ritual for thirty days and see how it improves your life.

If you were to implement one simple morning ritual, starting tomorrow, which one would make the biggest impact in your life?

To learn in more details how to create an exciting morning ritual, refer to my book, *Wake Up Call: How To Take Control of Your Morning And Transform Your Life.*

* * *

Action step

Using your action guide, create your own morning ritual including 2-3 simple daily habits. Then, commit to sticking to it for at least the next thirty days.

22

FIND PEOPLE WORTH FIGHTING FOR

 Life is not accumulation, it is about contribution.

— Stephen Covey, author, educator and businessman.

Whatever you are trying to accomplish, it's essential to have a strong reason for it to become a reality. There can be many reasons, such as:

- The benefits achieving your goals will give you. For instance, it might give you more freedom or autonomy and allow you to take care of your family.
- The benefits working on your goals will provide you. It might because you thoroughly enjoy what you're doing.

Your "why" can also be a person or a group of people. Having a strong desire to serve and make a difference in the lives of people around you might be an extremely powerful motivator for you. These beneficiaries may be your family members or a group of people you care about and want to help as much possible.

We have all heard stories of people who travelled the extra mile to help their loved ones. My questions for you are:

Who are you fighting for? Who are you trying to serve or help? Do you want to help homeless people? Starving children? Busy moms? Struggling entrepreneurs?

There is no shortage of people who need your help, and because you can always grow and develop new skills, you have the ability to serve others.

You'll find out that when you truly become obsessed with helping others, you'll have greater motivation and a deeper sense of purpose. You'll be excited about making a difference in other peoples' lives.

Thus, identify who you want to fight for. However, don't pick a group of people because it seems like the appropriate thing to do. Choose people that *you* have an interest in helping. It may be people with whom you share common values, or people you can relate to because you've been in their situation before. Whoever they may be, what matters is that you have a genuine desire to help them.

So, who will you be fighting for?

* * *

Action step

Answer the following questions, using your action guide:

- Who do I want to fight for?
- Who do I feel a strong desire to serve?

SECTION IV

LIVING IN INTEGRITY

Integrity is doing the right thing, even when no one is watching.

— C.S. LEWIS, WRITER AND THEOLOGIAN.

Do you assert yourself? Or do you let people walk all over you?

You didn't come to earth to be a doormat. You came to earth to express yourself to the fullest and live a life you can be proud of.

The point is, you must learn to respect yourself and your desires. Why? Because you matter.

Now, respecting yourself requires you to practice being honest with yourself so that you can make the difficult changes necessary to live the life you choose. It also entails you to practice being radically honest with others so you can build meaningful relationships that will benefit both you and your counterparts.

In this section, we'll discuss the key principles to adopt if you want to live life with integrity and feel good about yourself.

23

RESPECT YOURSELF

 Respect your efforts, respect yourself. Self-respect leads to self-discipline. When you have both firmly under your belt, that's real power.

— CLINT EASTWOOD, ACTOR AND FILMMAKER.

You matter. So, treat yourself as such!

Too often, we disrespect ourselves. We're nice with others and are willing to go the extra mile to help them, but we fail to do the same for ourselves. We neglect our values to allow us to fit in, we abandon our dreams to help other people achieve theirs, and we take care of others while forgetting to take care of ourselves.

But if we don't respect ourselves, why would others respect us? And how can we be loved if we don't love ourselves?

You must learn to respect yourself. It is only by respecting yourself that you can live your life according to your deepest values and aspirations. By doing so, you will make a bigger impact on the world around you. When you fail to respect yourself, you downplay your strengths, water down your personality and make yourself smaller than you really are. It might be tempting to pretend you don't matter, but is this true? Don't you risk losing yourself by acting this way?

Could fear be the reason you lack self-respect? Might you be running away from bigger, responsibilities, because you're scared of uncovering your greatness? Might you be scared of upsetting people by standing up for yourself?

You matter and, as such, should respect yourself and treat yourself as the important person you are. Respecting yourself actually means:

- Taking time for yourself each day,
- Trying to meet your needs on a regular basis,
- Being honest with yourself,
- Being assertive and asking for what you want, and
- Not being afraid to say "no".

The bottom line is, learn to respect yourself. Because if you don't, few people will. Respect yourself and acknowledge that who you are and what you do really matters.

* * *

Action step

What are three specific things you could do to show yourself more respect? Write them down in your action guide.

24

PRACTICE RADICAL HONESTY WITH YOURSELF

 If you want to be successful, you must respect one rule — never lie to yourself.

— PAULO COELHO, NOVELIST.

Are you honest with yourself or do you live in denial, being afraid to look at your own problems?

To achieve the results you want in life, you must look yourself in the mirror and face the harsh truth. Being aware is a prerequisite of change. So, what truths are you not telling yourself right now? In what ways could you be lying to yourself? For instance, do you pretend you're happy with your job when you're not? Do you tell yourself life is okay the way it is to avoid having to make difficult changes?

Now, it's unrealistic to expect to make every change you desire. And it's certainly not possible to work on everything at the same time. But are there some areas you've given up while pretending everything is okay? Perhaps it's related to your career. Perhaps it's in your relationships. Perhaps it's regarding your health.

Warning: Being brutally honest with yourself. What do you want that you don't yet have? And, what do you have that you're not willing to tolerate anymore?

* * *

Action step

Using your action guide, answer the questions below:

- Is my current life really what I want?
- What questions am I avoiding asking myself, and why?
- Knowing what I now know, if I could start all over, what would I do differently? What actions could I take now?
- If my future self—now five years older—were to talk to me, what would he/she tell me?
- Am I really doing whatever it takes to achieve the goals I say I want to achieve?

Warning: being radically honest with yourself doesn't mean beating yourself up. It means looking at your situation with honesty and asking yourself what you could do better.

25

PRACTICE RADICAL HONESTY WITH OTHERS

 Truth is the most valuable thing we have, so I try to conserve it.

— MARK TWAIN, WRITER AND HUMORIST.

How often do you gather the courage to say to others what you think and how you feel?

Being honest and telling others what we think is an extremely difficult thing to do. However, I believe it is essential. Here's what I mean by being radically honest:

1. Telling people how you really feel.
2. Telling people how they can improve.

1. Telling people how you feel

We're often afraid of sharing our feelings. We may be scared of people's reactions, or we may have too much pride or be unwilling to appear vulnerable. However, by failing to share our real feelings, we often build up resentment over time.

This is also unfair to the people we hide our feelings from. How can they adjust their behavior if they aren't even aware that they may be doing something that upsets us?

2. Telling people how they can improve

How often do you receive honest feedback from people around you?

We're usually unwilling to give honest feedback in case we hurt people. At least, that's the story we tell ourselves. But the truth is, we're often afraid of saying what we think because *we* don't want to be hurt. We fear being rejected. So, while on the one hand, we say we care about people, on the other hand, we deny them the right to know the truth as we see it. By doing so, we rob them of the opportunity to correct their behavior and improve the situation.

If you look back, you'll realize that it is often harsh feedback that allowed you to improve the most. And the only reason you could get such feedback is because others cared enough about you to tell you what they thought. These people believed in you and wanted you to improve. They were willing to take the risk to hurt you or to be rejected.

Being radically honest doesn't mean being rude or mean. You can— and I believe you should—give feedback in a gentle and respectful way. For example, you can tell people what they're doing well before suggesting the things they could improve upon. Then, you can end up with a compliment.

By being honest, you'll earn people's trust. By the same token, you will improve the quality of the relationship. Also, by sharing your feelings and giving honest feedback, you'll avoid building resentment, while giving others the opportunity to make positive changes.

So, when appropriate, practice being radically honest with others, not for the sake of being harsh with them, but because you care about them.

* * *

Action step

Using your action guide, answer the questions below:

- Who are you not sharing your honest feelings with?
- By failing to give people the honest feedback they deserve, who are you preventing from improving?

26

LEARN TO SAY NO

 Don't say maybe if you want to say no.

— Ryan Holiday, author and marketer.

No.

How do you say this word to reject people's invitations or requests?

You'll struggle to reach your true potential if you can't say no. If you're unable to decline other people's requests for your time, how will you deal with the incessant demands for your time when you're more successful? Successful people say no to almost everything which is (partly) why they're so successful.

How to say no

First, to say no effectively, you must know your values and goals. Otherwise, you risk saying yes to every opportunity or request. For any request, see whether it aligns with your priorities. Remember, your values and goals should dictate most of your decisions (see also *Chapter 12. Know what matters to you*).

For instance:

- Don't chase a promotion if you actually want to spend as much time as possible with your family.
- Stop going out every weekend if your priority is to create a successful side business.
- Avoid saying yes when deep down you want to say no.

Second, stop apologizing for the way you use your time. Nobody has the right to request your time without your permission. Doing so is selfish of them. Remember, giving up a chunk of your time is giving away a part of your life. Therefore, instead of saying "yes" all the time, make "no" your default answer. Accept requests only when you have a valid reason to do so.

Third, realize that valuing your time is a sign of self-respect. Standing up for your values and goals is giving them respect.

Finally, understand that to have the biggest impact possible on the world, you must be ruthless with the way you use your time. People-pleasers seldom reach their true potential because they fail to set their priorities and fight to protect them. Instead, they disrespect their time (and themselves) by saying yes to everything.

Don't be a doormat. Set your priorities. Value yourself enough to value your time. Then, use your time to achieve your biggest goals and make a positive impact on the world.

Note that I'm not saying you should never spend time helping other people. I'm saying you should learn to say no more often so that you can focus more effectively on your priorities. This way, you'll be more likely to achieve your goals.

Action step

If you could say "no" to anything without experiencing shame, guilt, or any other negative feelings, exactly what would you say no to? Write them all down in your action guide.

27

SET CLEAR RULES AND BOUNDARIES

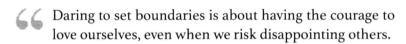 Daring to set boundaries is about having the courage to love ourselves, even when we risk disappointing others.

— BRENE BROWN, RESEARCH PROFESSOR AND AUTHOR.

Do you allow others to determine what your life should be like? Do you let people invade your personal space?

Being happy and successful requires you to respect yourself. When you don't, people will often take you for granted and use you to their advantage. This is why you must set clear boundaries so that people know what you will and, most importantly, will not tolerate.

Now, the exact nature of these rules and boundaries is entirely up to you. The only thing that matters is that they allow you to maintain your personal space, and they enable you to feel as though you're being true to yourself.

By setting clear boundaries and respecting them, you will feel better about yourself, and you will acquire a great sense of self-respect. Additionally, you will signal to others that you are a valuable person and should be treated as such (people won't be able to use you as their doormat anymore).

Another benefit of setting clear boundaries is that it will help you attract people who respect you—and your rules—while, at the same time, repelling people who don't. Put simply, your rules and boundaries will act as a powerful filter, inviting the right people into your life, while letting the others go.

Remember, if you don't decide how you want to be treated, people will treat you in whatever way *they* deem appropriate. The fewer boundaries you set the more people will tend to step over you. This is why you must "educate" people by showing them what is and isn't okay.

How to set boundaries

Below is a simple exercise to help you set healthy boundaries:

1. Write down the things you tolerate in your life, but you wish were different.
2. Establish clear rules you can stand behind. Then, write them down (be specific).
3. Imagine yourself acting according to your defined boundaries when the situation presents itself. To do so, rehearse your responses in your mind, using visualization.
4. Remind yourself that you have the right to set your own rules and boundaries and that not everyone will be happy about it.

* * *

Action step

Referring to the exercise above, decide on one specific rule you can implement to set clearer boundaries. It doesn't have to be anything big, but it should be specific and meaningful to you.

28

SHOW UP ON TIME

 It's really clear that the most precious resource we all have is time.

— STEVE JOBS, CO-FOUNDER OF APPLE, INC.

How many times have you been late in the past thirty days?

Time is one of your most valuable assets—as it is for everybody else. When you show up late or waste other people's time, you rob them of a fraction of their lives. By doing so, you show them a lack of respect.

This behavior not only shows how unreliable you are, but also how little you actually care for other people's time—at least that's what they will think. This will make it difficult to earn people's trust or respect.

From a business perspective, remember that every single dollar you'll ever earn, you'll earn it through people. You'll need people to trust you enough to part with their hard-earned money, and the first step on the road to earning their respect is to value their most precious asset—their time.

The point is, showing up on time is a sign of respect. It's the first step toward building trust. If you can't be on time, people might assume you'll slack off in other areas too.

During the first encounter with someone I'm considering working with, I give a lot of importance to details. Is the person on time? Did he or she complete the job I asked them to do properly? In general, people will work harder on their first job to secure the contract. Therefore, one small mistake at this early stage is a bad omen as it suggests they are likely to make more mistakes in the future.

This is precisely the way most people who want to work with you or hire you think. So, make sure you're reliable and give them a great first impression. And this starts by showing up on time.

With friends and family, being late might be fine, but for business-related meetings, always be punctual. If you can't, contact the person to let them know you'll be late in advance, if possible.

* * *

Action step

Strive to arrive on time (or earlier) to every business meeting in the next thirty days until it becomes a habit.

29

TAKE PRIDE IN YOUR WORK

 Big jobs usually go to the men who prove their ability to outgrow small ones.

— RALPH WALDO EMERSON, ESSAYIST AND PHILOSOPHER.

Do you take pride in your work?

You cannot always work on enjoyable tasks, but you always have control over the quality of the work you produce. You can choose to do your best, not just to please your boss or customers, but to please yourself. You are the one who chooses your standards and what you expect from yourself. As you continually attempt to do your best every day, you will most likely be given more responsibility over time.

People often say they would do more if they were paid more. While I understand this attitude, this way of thinking will seldom, if ever, lead to long-term success. It's only when you become "bigger" than your current line of work—and when this becomes obvious to everybody around you—that you will be put in a place that better matches your new skills. Perhaps you'll be promoted. Alternatively, you may decide to change companies or create your own business.

The point is, instead of waiting to be paid more to do more—do more. And in the mid to long term, you'll often earn yourself a pay hike. Do so not just to be paid more in the future, but, and perhaps more importantly, do it to feel good about yourself. After all, pride doesn't come from doing *less* than you know you're capable of doing, does it?

Therefore, immerse yourself in your work and strive to learn as much as possible about it. Before quitting your job, give it your best and keep improving. Raise your standards. You'll often find that the deeper you go—and the better you perform—the more enjoyable your job will become.

As you learn to take every job seriously and give it your best, you'll build the discipline, work ethic and attitude required to achieve a higher level of success in the future. Think about it this way: if you can't handle the tasks you're responsible for—no matter how small or unimportant they may seem—why would your boss, your company, the universe or anyone else ask you to handle more important tasks?

In summary, take pride in everything you do. Become bigger than your current environment by doing more than expected. Keep doing this over and over while applying the other success principles in this book and you'll more likely achieve your long-term career goals (along with your other goals).

* * *

Action step

Answer the following questions:

- Am I doing the best I can at work/school?
- If I were to step into my best self, what would I do differently?
- How can I become more engaged at work? What can I dive deeper into instead of running away from? Who can I interact with more often and at a deeper level?

30

CULTIVATE A PASSION FOR WHAT YOU DO

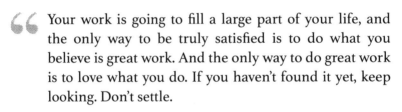 Your work is going to fill a large part of your life, and the only way to be truly satisfied is to do what you believe is great work. And the only way to do great work is to love what you do. If you haven't found it yet, keep looking. Don't settle.

— STEVE JOBS, CO-FOUNDER OF APPLE INC.

Do you go to work with excitement, or do you wake up with little to no motivation every day?

You're going to spend a big chunk of your life working. If we assume a conservative number of 1,500 working hours per year, you'll work 60,000 hours over a forty-year period. That's one heck of a lot of hours. How will you spend this time? Will you watch the clock over and over, waiting for the day to end, wishing you could be somewhere else, or will you immerse yourself in your work and let the time fly by?

When you do what you love, for the most part, work won't actually feel like work anymore. The emotional suffering you may currently experience from resisting work will simply fade away.

Let's face it, you won't always love every single thing you do at work. But if you find yourself spending the majority of your time working on unfulfilling tasks, I wouldn't recommend you keep doing it for the rest of your life.

In his book, *The Pathfinder*, Nicholas Lore mentioned an interesting survey. According to this survey, about 10% of the participants, who were all from the US, said they love their job. You can look at this survey in two ways. You can see the glass as half empty, thinking 10% isn't much. Alternatively, you can see it as half full, realizing that if 10% of people love their job—and that's millions of people in the US alone—you can, too.

I believe that designing a career you enjoy should be your priority. This is because it is impossible to separate your work from other areas of your life. Your work will affect your relationships with your family and friends, your health and your happiness. Loving what you do will often have a ripple effect that will positively impact other areas of your life. Conversely, having a job you hate can, over time, wreak havoc on other areas of your life.

In conclusion, it might be okay to spend a few years working at a soul-crushing job as a stopgap, but make sure these years don't turn into decades. Instead, be strategic and do what it takes to design a career you love. Remember, if there are people out there who love their job, why can't you be one of them?

So, identify your strengths and keep looking for things you find enjoyable and meaningful. Lean toward what you enjoy and *never* stop believing you can design a career you love.

To learn how to uncover your passion and start designing your dream career, refer to *The Passion Manifesto: Escape the Rat Race, Uncover Your Passion and Design a Career and Life You Love*

* * *

Action step

Answer the following questions:

- When do I feel the most engaged at work? What specifically am I doing in these moments?
- What do I volunteer for at work or outside of work? How can I do more of these things?

Additional step: choose one activity you enjoy and dedicate 10-15 minutes to pursuing it every day.

31

ASK FOR WHAT YOU WANT

 To be successful, you have to ask, ask, ask, ask, ask!

— JACK CANFIELD, SUCCESS COACH AND AUTHOR.

Do you ask for what you want?

Here is a simple truth: when you fail to ask, the answer is *always* no. Whatever we're trying to accomplish in this world, we cannot do it alone. We often hear about "self-made millionaires" who made it on their own, but this is a total myth. Whether we realize it or not, we constantly rely on other people's work and support in our day-to-day lives.

For instance, I wouldn't be able to do what I'm doing now if it weren't for Amazon and its hundreds of thousands of employees. And this is only possible by utilizing technologies such as the internet, and these had to be invented—guess what—by other people! What about the support I've received from my family and from countless other people I've met along the way?

My point is, you can't—and don't have to—do everything by yourself.

There are loads of people out there who have the knowledge, money or connections you need to turn your dreams into a reality.

Successful people ask for what they want. By doing so repeatedly, they automatically get an edge over people who don't. Just imagine if you asked for what you wanted all the time. Wouldn't you be more likely to get at least a few people to help you?

Unfortunately, when it comes to asking, we often hold onto limiting beliefs that prevent us from making the most of our ask-ability.

First, we are afraid of disturbing other people. If you find yourself in this situation, realize that most people love to help. It makes them feel useful, and perhaps even special. And who doesn't want to be useful?

Second, we don't want to appear selfish by having the "audacity" to ask for what we want. To make the asking process more natural, I invite you to practice unconditional giving. Whenever you can, help others. This will make it easier for you to reach out for help. It will also reduce the feeling you must reciprocate every time someone helps you (which can hold you back).

Third, we're unwilling to accept the idea that we actually need help. Let's face it, our pride often gets in the way. We want to do things by ourselves and appear strong. However, there are things you can't do because you never learned to. Why figure out things by yourself when you can ask people who have the skills or network to help you?

Fourth, we dread being rejected. Although being told "no" is never a pleasant experience, by not asking in the first place, we're robbing ourselves of countless opportunities to turn our dreams into reality. By avoiding potential rejections, we might be saying no to our biggest dreams and aspirations.

Yes, you *can* ask for what you want and, what's more, you'll receive it more often than you probably expect. Remember, when you fail to ask the answer is always no. So, stop saying no to your dreams. Like the success coach, Jack Canfield, put it, become an "askhole".

Ask, ask, ask. And then ask again.

* * *

Action step

This week, ask for one thing you want, whether it be small or big. For instance, you could ask for a discount, a small favor or an upgrade.

32

BE A PRODUCER, NOT A CONSUMER

 Your own reasons to make are reason enough. Create whatever causes a revolution in your heart.

— ELIZABETH GILBERT, AUTHOR.

Are you a producer or a consumer?

People who succeed in achieving all or most of their goals are proactive in the pursuit of their endeavors. Rather than spending their time glued to the TV, partying all weekend or going on shopping sprees, they take daily actions toward their dreams. Put differently, instead of consuming (information or materialistic things), they focus on producing. For instance, these people don't just:

- Read books, they write them,
- Listen to music, they write their own songs,
- Consume information, they produce content,
- Watch videos, they shoot them, or
- Talk about what they're going to do, they do it.

You can always consume later, once you have lots of time and/or money. But for now, it's absolutely critical you become a producer, *not a consumer*. As you learn to spend most of your time producing and putting into practice what you've learned, you'll start noticing tangible results in your life.

Also, as a human being, you will tend to be happier when you're fully engaged and using your creativity to express yourself. You can't truly express yourself by consuming. You must put yourself (and your soul) out there. And it starts by producing whatever you feel like putting out in the world. Perhaps you want to write books. Perhaps you want to sing. Perhaps you want to renovate your house.

Conversely, when you consume, you only experience temporary pleasure. For example, think of the thousands of hours you've spent in front of the TV in your life. How much value did you get from all these hours? Now, imagine if you had used at least some of this time to engage in productive activities that allowed you to express your creativity and unique personality? Wouldn't you feel better and proud of your creations?

To sum up, successful people tend to be producers. They continually think of ways to use their talents, skills and creativity to create. And they often use their free time to express themselves through their creations—rather than passively consuming information or products.

Decide today that you're going to become a producer and start creating. Remember, you are a creative being. When you fail to create, the result is often dissatisfaction or boredom.

So, what are you going to create, starting today? (See also *Chapter 69. Be a master, not a dabbler.*)

* * *

Action step

1. Answer the following questions:

- If I shifted from being a consumer to a producer, what would it mean to me?
- What can I do to better express my unique personality and creativity?

2. Using your action guide, write down one unproductive activity you regularly engage in. Then, write down one productive activity you could engage in instead.

SECTION V

CULTIVATING CONFIDENCE

With realization of one's own potential and self-confidence in one's ability, one can build a better world.

— DALAI LAMA, RELIGIOUS LEADER.

Do you truly believe in yourself? Do you have the inner confidence that you can achieve anything you set your mind to?

Most successful people have developed a high level of self-confidence over the years. This rock-solid confidence in themselves allows them to achieve many of the things they might previously have thought impossible.

To achieve your biggest goals and dreams, you too must develop confidence in yourself and in your vision.

Don't panic though. No matter how low your confidence may be, you can cultivate it and develop more confidence than you could have ever imagined. Confidence is a skill, and, like any other skill, it can be learned and developed. If you build self-confidence, everything will start changing for you. Let's see how you can do it, shall we?

33

BELIEVE YOU CAN

 Believe in yourself! Have faith in your abilities! Without a humble but reasonable confidence in your own powers you cannot be successful or happy.

— NORMAN VINCENT PEALE, MINISTER AND AUTHOR.

What you believe in strongly enough and for long enough will tend to become your reality. Therefore, the first step to achieving anything in life is to believe you can succeed. Believe that what you dream of doing is possible and it will be more likely to happen.

The act of believing activates your potential and unleashes your creativity. When you believe you can do something, you start asking yourself, "How? How am I going to do it?"

- How can I design my dream career?
- How can I meet the ideal partner?
- How can I retire early?
- How can I make more money?
- How can I get back in shape?

Your journey will only truly begin when you ask yourself "how".

Successful people ask themselves better questions and, as a result, achieve better results. Be one of them. Ask yourself smart questions that help you achieve your goals. Also, understand that if someone else can achieve something, so can you. This has been my mantra for the past few years. I never stopped believing I could become a full-time writer. Eventually, it became my reality.

Remember, belief is the invisible force that turns the intangible—your thoughts—into the tangible—specific objects or measurable results. As such, belief is your most valuable currency. Use it to attract success, health and wealth into your life.

Believe you can. Then, sustain that belief over a long period of time while taking consistent action daily toward your vision. Keep looking for people who have achieved your goals. Do what they do. Think the way they think. Study what they study, and continually remind yourself every day that *you can*.

The key message is this: developing a rock-solid belief in your ability to achieve your goals is one of the most powerful things you can do to transform your life. If someone else can achieve something, most likely, you can achieve it too. So, keep believing that what you want is possible.

* * *

Action step

- Select one of your biggest goals or dreams and allow yourself to believe you can achieve it.
- Write down all the reasons you believe so.
- Write down all the things you could do to start moving toward that goal.
- Imagine you have already achieved this goal. Then, relax and allow yourself to feel good about it.

34

BELIEVE THAT WHO YOU ARE AND WHAT YOU DO MATTERS

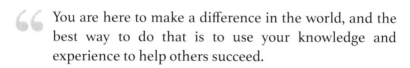 You are here to make a difference in the world, and the best way to do that is to use your knowledge and experience to help others succeed.

— BRENDON BURCHARD, AUTHOR AND HIGH-
PERFORMANCE COACH.

Nothing is more disempowering than to believe that who you are and what you do doesn't matter. Sadly, society often likes to remind you how "powerless" you (supposedly) are:

- Politicians want you to see yourself as a victim so that they can pose as the saviors.
- Economists tell you the economy is bad and that there is nothing you can do about it.
- Religious gurus ask you to bow at their feet and believe everything they say.
- Philosophers lecture you on how you're supposed to think.
- Marketers make you feel insecure or needy so that you buy the products they want to sell you.

Here is the thing: it's easier to manipulate people when they believe they are powerless. However, the truth is, you have far more power than you realize. History has shown that a few determined individuals can influence millions upon millions of people.

Do you realize there will never be another person exactly like you? You have unique personality traits, talents and skills. Consequently, it is your responsibility to cultivate these skills so that you can improve both your life and the lives of the people around you.

You matter because you can always decide to help other people, regardless of your present situation. You might not see the impact of your actions, but it doesn't mean there isn't any. I will never hear from most of my readers, yet I know that my work will impact the lives of some of them. In turn, these people will touch the lives of others around them, thereby creating further positive ripples in the world.

The point is, you matter. You *can* make a difference in the world. So, take responsibility for your actions, embrace your destiny, and go create awesome positive ripples in this world. Because, if you don't, who else will?

* * *

Action step

- Close your eyes. Then, allow yourself to let go of any need for approval (from your parents, friends, colleagues, society et cetera). Imagine how freeing it will be if you don't need to prove anything to anyone.
- Appreciate yourself just for existing and acknowledge your inherent value as an individual human being with a unique personality.
- Think of all the people you've ever helped in even the smallest way.
- Feel good for being you.

35

CHALLENGE YOUR LIMITING BELIEFS

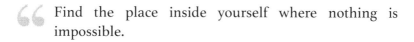 Find the place inside yourself where nothing is impossible.

— DEEPAK CHOPRA, AUTHOR.

I have bad news for you. You've been programmed.

During your childhood, you've been told lies over and over, and these have led you to adopt the false beliefs that now determine what you believe you can and can't do. This is because your parents have transmitted to you their fears and limitations. So did your friends, your family members and your teachers.

Here is the truth: most of your beliefs aren't actually yours. They are other people's beliefs, which you adopted mostly unconsciously. You are largely the product of your environment. The good news is that you can reprogram your mind and implement any empowering belief you desire. Indeed, the latest research in neuroscience has shown that you can, at any age, create new neural connections in your brain. As a result, you can change the way you feel, think, and act.

Never forget that what you believe will, for the most part, determine the results you will attain in life. Disempowering beliefs will lead to poor results and lack of fulfillment, but powerful beliefs will lead to positive results and enhanced happiness. So, why not start adopting empowering beliefs that support your goals?

Let's have a look at a simple process you can use to eliminate your limiting beliefs and replace them with empowering ones.

* * *

Action step

Here is a simple step-by-step process to overcome your limiting beliefs:

1. Select one area of your life and ask yourself why you're not at a 10/10 in this area.
2. Look at all the reasons (or excuses) you came up with.
3. Challenge them. Are they really true? Write down any counter argument you can think of.
4. Find specific examples that disprove each of these reasons or beliefs (whether in your personal life or in other people's lives) and write them down.
5. Choose the empowering belief you want to adopt instead.
6. Create an affirmation using the tips below:

- Use present tense,
- Use the first person, and
- Make it specific and keep it short.

For instance, if you believe you don't have enough time, you could use the affirmation below:

"I always make the time to do whatever I'm committed to."

36

FOCUS ON WHAT YOU WANT

 The key to success is to focus our conscious mind on things we desire, not things we fear.

— BRIAN TRACY, AUTHOR AND MOTIVATIONAL SPEAKER.

How much energy do you waste focusing on what you fear or on what you don't want?

This is wasted energy you will never get back.

Why not focus on what you want instead? I invite you to keep thinking about what you desire the most. Focus on what you want when you wake up in the morning. When you brush your teeth, think about what excites you. When you go to bed, visualize your ideal future. Continually and repeatedly focus on what you want. Be there in your mind weeks, months, or years before it actually happens.

Understand that your focus drives your actions. When you focus on what you fear, you put yourself in a negative state that prevents you from taking action. You start doubting yourself and may end up giving up on your goals.

For example, constantly worrying about your business or financial situation won't help you. Do you think Thomas Edison would have succeeded at inventing the light bulb if he kept dwelling on all his "failures"? It took him thousands of attempts before he succeeded, but he never stopped focusing on the results he wanted to achieve, which enabled him to persevere.

Your ability to maintain a positive state of mind as you move toward what you desire the most is key to achieving any of your goals.

Therefore, like Edison, you must cultivate the habit of focusing on what you want until it becomes your reality.

Want to make more money? Rather than focusing on your lack of finances, be grateful for all the amazing things you already have in your life. Then, get excited about creating more wealth in the future. Surround yourself with wealthy people. Read books written by wealthy people. Keep learning anything you can about how to earn money.

Want to become an amazing speaker? Rather than focusing on your poor communication skills, visualize yourself on the stage delivering an inspiring speech. Read stories of people who went from being terrified of public speaking to becoming world-class orators. Focus your attention on your desire to become a great speaker and keep practicing, both in your mind and in the real world.

What I'm saying is, focus on what you have and what you want, *not* on what you don't have and what you don't want. By doing so, you will maintain the positive emotional state needed to take the inspired actions that move you toward your goals.

* * *

Action step

- Select one thing you want.
- Join at least one group of people moving toward the same goal, either online or offline.

- For the next seven days:
- Write three things you are grateful for related to that thing.
- Spend a few minutes every day reading books and articles on the topic.
- Take one small action to move closer to your goal.

37

CULTIVATE OPTIMISM

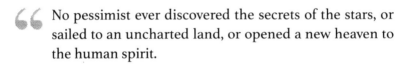 No pessimist ever discovered the secrets of the stars, or sailed to an uncharted land, or opened a new heaven to the human spirit.

— HELEN KELLER, AUTHOR AND POLITICAL ACTIVIST.

Is your glass half full or half empty?

It is easy to lose enthusiasm when things don't go as planned, but in every "failure" lies a learning opportunity. You can make the most of any setback by learning from it or you can keep complaining, whining, and crying about it.

The major problem with pessimism is that it doesn't improve your life in any way. This is because, instead of cultivating happiness and practicing gratitude, pessimists direct their focus toward all the things that do go or could go wrong.

That said, being an optimist doesn't mean ignoring your problems. It means acknowledging reality and deciding to focus on its positive aspects while avoiding wasting time and energy on its negative ones. In a nutshell, it means feeding the good and starving the bad.

When you focus on the positive and look for constructive solutions, you activate your creativity and boost your emotional state. And, as we've seen before, keeping a positive state of mind is an essential tool to help you design a happy and successful life.

The key point is, feeling sorry for yourself and blaming reality for being "real" will never allow you to realize your potential, design a remarkable life and achieve your most exciting goals. So, learn to cultivate optimism. Choose to focus on the positive side of things as often as possible. Practice gratitude every day. Visualize the ideal outcome you want to create and reframe every situation by giving it an empowering meaning that serves you well.

Finally, accept that short-term failures are inevitable but remain optimistic as you move toward your vision. As you do so, you will be amazed at what you will accomplish in the long run.

In *Section IX. Developing emotional resilience*, we'll discuss in greater depth how you can become more resilient.

* * *

Action step

Answer the following question:

What are two or three specific things you could do to cultivate a greater sense of optimism?

38

PERCEIVE THE OPPORTUNITIES
AROUND YOU

> A pessimist is one who makes difficulties of his opportunities and an optimist is one who makes opportunities of his difficulties.

— Harry S Truman, former president of the United States.

Do you look for opportunities or argue for limitations?

Successful people are busy exploiting opportunities, while skeptics argue it can't be done. In our hyperconnected world, opportunities are plentiful. And when we account for the unlimited number of ideas we can generate, options become endless.

Spotting opportunities is a skill you can develop over time. It begins by being open-minded, looking for what *could be* rather than what *is*. To do so, you must let go of your disbelief and allow yourself to dream.

Don't worry, though. There is no need to have earth-shattering ideas or to possess the skills or confidence to make these ideas come true—at least not yet. For now, you only need to practice thinking in terms of possibilities. Remember, before you can do anything you must believe it to be possible. Therefore, avoid being a skeptic or a naysayer. Instead, maintain an open mind at all times.

Then, learn to ask yourself the correct questions to identify opportunities.

- What are the current trends?
- Which industries are growing?
- In which direction is the world evolving?
- What needs are left unmet in the marketplace?
- What skills do I have and how can I use them effectively?

Millions of people have issues, and these people need someone to help solve them. As long as human beings have problems, there will always be plenty of opportunities to help.

One of the best ways to find opportunities is to continually look for ways to make things better. Are you frustrated with a certain service? Do you think you could do a better job? Do you have an idea you believe could work?

When I started self-publishing books on Amazon, I realized I could offer books that would be practical, easy to read and concise, and I could sell them at a cheaper price than traditionally published books. I was told the market was saturated. However, I looked at successful indie authors, thinking I could do even better. In short, I saw an opportunity and chose to pursue it, believing I had the strengths and passion required for success.

Of course, everybody has ideas. The key is to become exceptional at executing them. We'll see how to do that in *Section VI. Developing an accurate model of reality* and *Section VII. Getting things done*

The bottom line is, instead of living in fear and scarcity, acknowledge the sea of opportunities around you. While you do so, keep working on yourself. The better your attitude and skills are, the more opportunities will appear.

* * *

Action step

1. Ask yourself the following questions:

- What can be improved around me?
- What do I need to learn, in order for new opportunities to open up for me?
- What opportunities are so obvious that I may have missed them?

2. Ask someone close to you what opportunities they see for you.

3. Write down ten new ideas each morning on any topic of interest.

39

THINK BIG

 Big thinkers are specialists in creating positive, forward-looking, optimistic pictures in their own minds and in the minds of others. To think big, we must use words and phrases that produce big, positive mental images.

— DAVID J. SCHWARTZ, MOTIVATIONAL WRITER AND COACH.

Have you ever downsized your goals because you thought they were impossible to reach?

There is nothing wrong with breaking down your goals into smaller tasks. However, this doesn't mean downsizing them. When you refuse to chase your biggest goals, you risk setting suboptimal goals that don't excite you, and excitement is what starts you moving. Without a burning desire to turn your vision into reality, you may find yourself procrastinating, taking far less action than you should. This will often lead to mediocre results.

Consequently, rather than worrying about your goals being too big, concentrate on the excitement they generate. The more excited you are, the better. If you can't stop thinking of a goal or idea for weeks or months, perhaps there is a reason for it. So, why not take a small step and begin your journey?

Now, you don't need to take insane risks. Simply take the smallest step you can think of, whether it is doing research, buying a book, or sending an email to an acquaintance. Lean toward your dreams and observe what happens when you do.

Think big, start small

The key is to think big but start small. No matter how huge your vision happens to be, in the long term, only the consistent completion of simple daily tasks will get you there. This is why thinking "too big" isn't the problem—not starting small by breaking down your goals is.

Another reason to think big is because pursuing ambitious goals requires you to become a better person. Among other things, you will have to boost your confidence, build stronger self-discipline and skyrocket your ability to persevere. As the business philosopher, Jim Rohn, put it, "The real value isn't in the goal but in the person you're becoming in the process of achieving that goal."

So, think big and stop selling yourself short. Think big to become a bigger person—the person you were meant to be. You might not achieve your loftiest vision, but you'll become a better person in the process, and nobody will ever be able to take that away from you.

Action step

- Envision the craziest and most unrealistic dreams you can think of.
- Think of the smallest action you could take to move closer to those dreams.
- Take that small action today and see where it takes you.

40

BELIEVE YOU WILL IMPROVE
LONG-TERM

 You must expect great things of yourself before you can do them.

— MICHAEL JORDAN, FORMER PROFESSIONAL BASKETBALL
PLAYER.

Do you often feel inadequate?

When things don't go your way, it's easy to lose sight of the big picture and start feeling unworthy of your biggest aspirations. However, instead of feeling sorry for yourself, I encourage you to cultivate a "growth mindset". That is, to believe you can become better over time.

This subtle shift from "I'm not good enough" to "I'm exactly where I'm supposed to be right now and will become better over time" can make all the difference in the world.

We dramatically underestimate our ability to improve over time. The truth is, almost everything is learnable by almost anybody. Now, I'm not saying you will become the best in the world, but you can become proficient, if not excellent, at most of the things you're willing to put time and effort into learning. Some of the best speakers in the world used to be socially awkward. Outstanding salesmen were once the worse in their company, and exceptional authors were sometimes told they should give up on writing.

Fortunately, our mind is so powerful it can learn almost anything. Do you remember your first driving lesson? I'm betting it seemed so complicated that you likely felt overwhelmed, worried you'd never be able to drive. But what happened next? Through practice, your subconscious mind took over. You internalized "driving" and it became second nature. Well, I have good news: you can do the same with any other skill.

Did you know chess players can memorize the positions of all pieces on the board almost instantly? Now, can you guess what happens when you put the chess pieces randomly on the board? The same chess players can't remember the position of the pieces any better than you and me. Why is that? Simply because pieces put randomly on a chessboard don't form any known patterns.

The point is, you don't need to be good enough (yet) because you can always improve in the long term. The way you do this is by internalizing patterns through practice and repetition. So, instead of feeling inadequate, realize you can always improve, and with practice and effort, you inevitably will.

* * *

Action step

1. Look at one of the things you can do well.
2. Remember a time where you couldn't do that thing.
3. Think of something you want to become great at.
4. Assume mastering that thing is inevitable in the mid to long term.

41

CELEBRATE YOUR SUCCESS

 The more you praise and celebrate your life, the more there is in life to celebrate.

— OPRAH WINFREY, TALK SHOW HOST AND TELEVISION
PRODUCER.

Success is a process consisting of ups and downs. You can ignore your achievements and beat yourself up every time you face setbacks, or you can celebrate your small successes and let your setbacks teach you valuable lessons. Which option do you think will help you persevere and thrive in the long run?

We're generally good at pointing out our failures and shortcomings, but we often fail to acknowledge all our little accomplishments. With this type of behavior, it's no wonder we often feel bad about ourselves.

As you cultivate the habit of celebrating your successes, even the tiniest ones, you'll be able to maintain a more positive emotional state. You'll become your own coach and feel inspired to persevere. And this positive state of mind will allow you to persevere in spite of the multiple setbacks you'll probably face along the way.

There is no such thing as failure, only feedback. The key is to learn from each of your so-called failures. This is what the process called success is all about. So, make sure you acknowledge what doesn't work, i.e., your "failures". Then, use them as feedback to make the necessary adjustments until you achieve your goal.

Expecting to reach any goal without encountering setbacks is unrealistic and goes against the nature of reality. We learn through practice. It is how we receive feedback from reality and learn to separate what works from what doesn't. So, develop the habit of celebrating successes and, every single day, think of three things you did well. Keep looking for ways to acknowledge your progress. Then, take more action in the direction of your goals. Finally, realize that short-term failures are inevitable and learn from each of them to the best of your ability.

There is no failure, only invaluable feedback leading to long-term success (see also *Chapter 76. Make the most of your mistakes* and *Chapter 81. Leverage the power of reframing*).

To learn how to build motivation and sustain it over the long term, you can refer to the second book in the Mastery Series, *Master Your Motivation: A Practical Guide to Unstick Yourself, Build Momentum and Sustain Long-Term Motivation*.

* * *

Action step

At the end of your day, ask yourself:

"What are the three things I'm most proud of having done today?"

42

MOVE BEYOND YOUR COMFORT ZONE

 All our dreams can come true, if we have the courage to
pursue them.

— WALT DISNEY, ENTREPRENEUR AND FILM PRODUCER.

Your ability to uncover your potential is proportional to the amount
of discomfort you're willing to experience. Muscles don't grow unless
they're put under intense pressure. The same goes for you. You'll
never discover what you're capable of achieving if you refuse to face
your fears.

Ultimately, fears are illusions, and the only way you'll realize this is
by taking action. When in contact with reality, fears will disappear.
Why? Because fears are products of the mind and, for the most part,
they are irrational. They cannot stand the test of reality.

Have you ever faced a fear just to realize it wasn't such a big deal after
all? Perhaps, as you did so, you even experienced a sense of euphoria.
I believe this is your inner self rewarding you for your courage and
encouraging you to expand beyond your present self.

There is no telling what you can do when you continuously push past your fears. In the history of humankind, people with a strong purpose and a burning desire to find their true nature and overcome their fears have gone on to impact the lives of countless people. Therefore, never assume you can't do something. Instead, remember you can always improve. You *can* overcome your fears.

If you want to find out how far can you go, start by leaving your comfort zone. You cannot reach a higher level of success by only doing familiar things. To grow, you must embrace discomfort and develop a higher self-concept. You must see yourself for who you can become and demand more from yourself.

A comfort zone may be a beautiful place, but nothing ever grows there. So, little by little, start facing your fears and let reality show you how unreal these fears are—and let it show you how much more you can become.

Below are some tips to help you move beyond your comfort zone:

- **Start small.** Do something a little scary to start building confidence and momentum. For instance, instead of delivering a speech, record a video of yourself delivering your speech.
- **Do the impossible.** Challenge yourself to do one thing you thought impossible for you. It could be giving a speech, learning a specific skill or cold calling a prospect.
- **Get support.** You don't have to do things alone. Surround yourself with people who have already achieved your goal. Also, have someone to hold you accountable, which will make it easier for you to take the action you said you would.

Action step

Complete the following exercises below, using your action guide:

1. What does "moving beyond your comfort zone" mean to you?
2. Remember one time you pushed beyond your comfort zone. How did it make you feel?
3. Think of one uncomfortable thing you could do today or later this week and decide to undertake it.

43

PRACTICE POSITIVE SELF-TALK

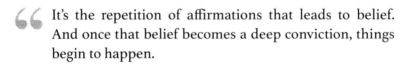 It's the repetition of affirmations that leads to belief. And once that belief becomes a deep conviction, things begin to happen.

— MUHAMMAD ALI, WORLD CHAMPION BOXER AND

ACTIVIST.

Would you talk to someone you love the same way you talk to yourself?

Most of us have developed the toxic habit of talking ourselves down. We use every single mistake as a reason to disrespect ourselves. We tell ourselves how stupid, careless or lazy we are. We insult, belittle, and mentally harass ourselves. If you talked to others the same way you talk to yourself, you would probably be arrested for psychological abuse.

The way you talk to yourself determines how you feel and act. This is why positive self-talk is a major component of happiness and success. Sure, you can be harsh on yourself and still achieve external success, but what will be the cost to your mental health?

Some people believe they won't accomplish anything significant unless they beat themselves up. However, this is a myth. It's not true. People who "succeed" by being harsh on themselves, most likely succeed *in spite* of criticizing themselves—not *because* of it.

Think about it. Would you enjoy having a coach constantly telling you what a loser you are, or would you prefer a coach who encourages you to become the best you can be?

You have a choice: you can "motivate" yourself by using fear, or you can use inspiration, love and self-compassion. I recommend you experiment with the latter and see how much better you feel.

How to practice positive self-talk

Talking to yourself in a gentle way is a habit that anybody can develop with enough practice. Below are a few tips to help you do that:

- **Adopt empowering mantras.** Repeat the affirmations you came up with before (see *Chapter 35. Challenge your limiting beliefs*) or create new ones.
- **Consume inspirational materials.** Spend at least a few minutes each day to absorb uplifting content. Whenever you find a sentence or quote you like, note it down somewhere. Over time, you'll come up with positive mantras that will serve you well in moments of doubt.
- **Listen to positive self-talk.** Search for "positive self-talk" videos on YouTube. Then, find a soundtrack you like and listen to it every morning for thirty days in a row.

Keep feeding your mind with a healthy dose of positivity. As you do so, you'll start changing your outlook on life, which will positively impact how you feel and act.

Since you have to be with yourself 24/7, make your own company a pleasant experience.

* * *

Action step

For 24 hours, observe your self-talk. How is the little voice inside you treating you? Notice when you criticize yourself and what impacts it has on your mental well-being.

44

PRACTICE VISUALIZATION

 Live out of your imagination, not your history.

— STEPHEN R. COVEY, AUTHOR, EDUCATOR AND
BUSINESSMAN.

When you think about your future, do you visualize the best or expect the worse?

The thing that differentiates human beings from any other living creatures is our ability to imagine something before it actually happens. We can rehearse a speech, see ourselves being confident at a meeting, or practice free throws. And we can do all these things in our mind as many times as we want without anyone being able to stop us. Amazing, isn't it?

As such, your imagination is one of your most valuable assets. It's more powerful than your willpower. Many successful people continuously visualize the future they want to create. They see themselves succeeding in various areas of their lives over and over again. They have an exciting vision and they can't wait to turn it into reality. Now, they don't just daydream about an ideal future, they clearly visualize what they want with the firm intent and the inner belief that it *will* become their reality.

In truth, your mind cannot tell the difference between an actual experience and an imagined one. As a result, by using visualization, you can practice being the person you want to be. You can see yourself being confident, perseverant, or courageous. You can visualize practicing a speech, rehearsing a play, or playing the piano. Over time, as you keep envisioning yourself being the person you want to be, you will start acting accordingly. Many CEOs, athletes, and musicians use visualization to boost their performance.

- CEOs visualize how they want to conduct a meeting. Or they keep thinking of their vision which enables them to better convince stakeholders to support them.
- Athletes see themselves performing at their best and hold this image in their mind as they're about to begin their performance.
- Musicians see themselves playing their instruments with grace and skill.

Visualization is one of your most powerful tools. Use it every day to design your ideal life, not to dwell on the past or worry about the future (see also *Chapter 50. Focus on solutions,* and *Chapter 36. Focus on what you want*).

* * *

Action step

Take a couple of minutes now to visualize yourself in a specific situation. It can be a future goal you want to achieve or an uncomfortable situation you want to handle better. See yourself feeling, thinking, and acting the way you want to.

SECTION VI

DEVELOPING AN ACCURATE MODEL OF REALITY

It ain't what you don't know that gets you into trouble. It's what you know for sure that just ain't so.

— MARK TWAIN, WRITER AND HUMORIST.

Do you fight against reality, believing things should be the way you want them to be? Do you think you should be rewarded just because you do superb work or because you care deeply?

This is not how life works. Reality obeys certain laws. When you closely align with reality and do things that work in the real world, you'll increase the likelihood of achieving your goals. But when you ignore reality and try to do things your own way, you will most likely fail to design the life you desire.

This is why successful people strive to align themselves with reality. They don't fantasize about a hypothetical future or merely daydream, they observe reality and dissect it to further their understanding of the way it works.

For instance, to reach any of their goals, successful people make a conscious effort to find out what they must do in the real world to close the gap between where they are and where they need to be. They don't rely on luck. Instead, they look for role models, search for effective blueprints and question their own assumptions and limitations. In short, they strive to think and act the best possible way to maximize their chances of reaching their goals. This is what I like to refer to as, "developing an accurate model of reality".

People who are able to develop a fairly accurate model of reality are more likely to take the appropriate actions and achieve their goals. People who can't, will often take little to no action or waste their time taking action that produces no tangible results. Therefore, if you are serious about achieving your major goals, you must refine your model of reality and develop a more accurate one.

In this section, we'll see how you can deepen your understanding of reality so that you can start developing a better model. Let's get started.

45

UNDERSTAND THAT SUCCESS IS A PROCESS

 Patience is a key element of success.

— BILL GATES, CO-FOUNDER OF MICROSOFT CORP.

To develop an accurate model of reality you must understand that success is a process, not an event. You don't achieve success by taking a few actions, believing you'll make it big because your work is so incredible. No.

Success is a result of consistent hard work done strategically (almost) every day and sustained over a long period of time.

The key point here, is that your hard work must be aligned with your overall strategy. That is, you must:

1. Determine the best way to travel from where you are to where you want to be,
2. Identify the key tasks to be included in the process, and
3. Stick to these tasks long enough to achieve the results you desire (while avoiding doing anything that works against your strategy).

A strategy is valuable not just because it tells you what to do, but also because it tells you what *not* to do. Sadly, instead of relying on a sound strategy, many people fall for short-term gimmicks, get-rich schemes, or short-lived tactics.

For instance, an author may post inspirational quotes on Facebook, experiment with Facebook lives, dabble with YouTube videos or publish articles on various blogs. While there is nothing wrong with any of these activities, unless they are part of a crystal-clear strategy, they will mostly be a waste of time and energy.

The lesson here is that everything you do must be based on your strategy. Your strategy is the compass that guides you and prevents you from getting lost along the way.

Remember, success is a process. It results from establishing a clear strategy, identifying your key tasks, and working on them consistently over a long period of time. It is *not* a single event. So, stop hoping you'll be a success one day. Instead, put a clear strategy in place and create a specific action plan to work from.

So, what specific process will enable you to achieve success in the long term?

Action step

1. Select one meaningful goal you want to achieve.
2. Identify the best process to help you reach that goal. What daily habits could you implement? What key tasks would you focus on?

46

ALIGN YOURSELF WITH REALITY

 Most people treat the present moment as if it were an obstacle that they need to overcome. Since the present moment is life itself, it is an insane way to live.

— ECKHART TOLLE, WRITER AND SPIRITUAL TEACHER.

Do you want reality to be different than it is?

Stop.

If you argue against reality, you will lose every time. Reality doesn't care about your feelings, beliefs, or predictions. Neither does it care how hard you work nor how noble your intentions happen to be. If you try to be successful using methods that are out of alignment with reality, you will keep struggling and will most likely never achieve your goals.

Consequently, understanding the way reality works is critical. Once you grasp the rules of the game, the game becomes easier to play—and positive results become easier to achieve. I believe "aligning with reality" means the following:

- Continuously trying to identify what works and what doesn't (by learning all you can from the most knowledgeable people in that field),
- Getting feedback from reality through repeated testing,
- Keeping an open mind and avoiding making inaccurate assumptions that will lead to poor decisions (see also *Chapter 51. Don't assume, verify*),
- Having the courage to look at your failures and learn from them (rather than being in denial), and
- Becoming an acute observer of reality to refine your model of reality (and make better decisions).

The more accurate your model becomes, the more likely you are to be successful in your endeavors. Think about it this way: deluded people seldom reach their goals. You probably know such people. They are the ones telling you how they're going to achieve X, Y, Z. The problem is, they don't understand what it takes nor how to do it. So, make sure you upgrade your model of reality and put in place a strategy to maximize your chances of achieving your goals.

Reality is never wrong, but your approach can often be.

To learn in more detail how to align yourself with reality and achieve tangible results, refer to the fifth book in the Mastery Series, *Master Your Thinking: A Practical Guide to Align Yourself with Reality and Achieve Tangible Results in the Real World*

* * *

Action step

Reflect on the two questions below in relation to your previous goal:

- In what ways am I trying to fight against reality?
- How does it make me feel?

SEE FAILURES AS PART OF THE PROCESS

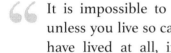 It is impossible to live without failing at something, unless you live so cautiously that you might as well not have lived at all, in which case you have failed by default.

— J. K. ROWLING, NOVELIST.

I despise the word "failure". Thinking in terms of failure is not only inaccurate but also highly disempowering. In fact, so-called failures are entirely part of the process we call success. They are not separate from it. By repeatedly trying and failing, we learn to separate what works from what doesn't (i.e., we improve our model of reality).

Thus, it is unrealistic, if not silly, to expect to do well the first time we attempt anything new. Yet, this is what many people do. They hold unrealistic expectations, and when their expectations clash with reality—and they will—these people tend to feel disappointed and give up. They consider themselves as "not smart enough" or "out of luck". However, this is not how reality works. Success is a process created from trial and error. Your brain needs feedback—failure—if it is to learn. How do you expect to learn otherwise?

If you fail to reframe the way you perceive failure, you'll struggle to become proficient at anything. You'll keep giving up, trying one thing after another, hoping to find something you're skilled at. By all means, spend time identifying your strengths and talents and make the most of them, but never expect to be good at everything from the get-go (see also *Chapter 13. Know your strengths*).

Here is a personal example of this principle. I'm a member of Toastmasters, a non-profit organization for people who want to practice public speaking. The other day, one of the members made a speech on grit. He explained how scared he was of public speaking and how often he considered giving up. It's wonderful he could overcome that. But, to be honest, I find it odd. Why would someone give up after a few speeches because they still have stage fright or aren't as competent as they expected? It takes hundreds of speeches to become a decent public speaker and probably thousands to become an excellent one. Expecting things to be any other way is unrealistic.

Successful people see failure as inevitable. As such, they are willing to fail as many times as necessary until they eventually achieve their goals. In other words, they approach challenges with a much more realistic approach. Let me say it again. You will *never* become excellent at anything unless you are willing to fail and learn from those failures. There is no way you can reach your full potential any other way. You must keep trying and learning. You must refine your model of reality *until* you achieve your goals.

Aim to fail more than anybody else you know, and in the long term, you will succeed beyond your expectations.

* * *

Action step

In which areas of your life are you not trying and failing enough? If you weren't afraid of failure, what would you do differently in those areas?

48

LOOK FOR ROLE MODELS

 Success leaves clues.

— TONY ROBBINS, AUTHOR AND LIFE COACH.

On your journey toward success, you have two options. You can:

1. Try to figure out everything on your own, or
2. Follow the steps of people who have already achieved the results you want.

Which option do you think works better?

The key to achieving your goals is to absorb the mindset, beliefs and habits of the people you are trying to emulate. To do so, you need to dissect their strategy and find out what they did to gain success. How did they create their successful businesses, build powerful muscles or retire early?

Thus, instead of reinventing the wheel, spend time with people who have what you want and can help you get it. By "spend time", I don't necessarily mean face to face, but I mean by immersing yourself in their work. You could do this by watching their YouTube videos, reading their books or buying their courses. Or, even better, by having them mentor you or coach you (if possible).

Let your role models' success inspire you. Keep believing it's possible for you to emulate their success, too. Because if others can succeed at something, you most likely can as well. Meanwhile, stay away from the naysayers and cynics who will drain your energy and make you doubt yourself. Keep looking up to your role models and adopt their habits. Learn as much as you can from them and never stop improving until you achieve the results you want.

Remember, a massive component of success results from your ability to remain optimistic even when things don't go your way. A positive attitude will keep you going until you achieve the breakthroughs you're looking for (see also *Chapter 33. Believe you can*, and *37. Cultivate Optimism*). One of the reasons I was able to transition into writing full-time was because I kept looking at other successful indie writers, knowing that if they could do it, I could do it, too

The bottom line is, surround yourself with role models, whether physically or virtually. Learn from them and maintain an unshakable belief in yourself as you move toward your highest goals.

* * *

Action step

Identify one or two people who have already achieved the meaningful goal you're chasing. Then, resolve to learn everything you can from them.

49

DRAMATICALLY REDUCE YOUR LEARNING CURVE

 It's what you learn after you know it all that counts.

— JOHN WOODEN, BASKETBALL PLAYER AND COACH.

Your time on this earth is limited. Thus, you must continuously endeavor to reduce your learning curve. Stop doing what your friends—or most people—do. They probably have poor strategies and move way too slowly. Instead, look for ways to achieve your goals as rapidly as possible. Discover what the most productive people on earth actually do. Ask yourself:

- How can I achieve that goal as quickly as possible and with as little effort as possible?
- Who has the best blueprint for that specific goal?
- If I were to perform certain specific key tasks every day, consistently, which ones are most likely to guarantee my success?

By spending time looking for the best approach, you'll save yourself a lot of time down the road (in some cases, months or even years). Remember, if you're serious about achieving your goal, you must put in place the best strategy possible. Avoid jumping headfirst into action. Instead, map out a detailed plan. Note that your plan doesn't have to be perfect, since you can always refine it as you go along.

Here are a couple of additional tips:

Follow people who actually walk the talk. Finding the best course of action is not always easy. An effective way to reduce noise is to ensure you learn from people who've actually been there and done that. For instance, while there are tons of courses on how to self-publish, only a handful are from writers who actually make a comfortable living from their writing. These are the best courses out there, in my opinion.

Don't assume, research. Don't assume that because your friends are doing it, it's the most effective approach. Don't buy into the general consensus. Remember, most people aren't wildly successful, so why would you emulate them? Let go of your assumptions and keep an open mind. You can often learn faster than you think (see also *Chapter 51. Don't assume, verify* and *Chapter 54. Challenge the status quo*).

Your time is limited, so don't try to reinvent the wheel.

Action step

Answer the following questions about your goal:

- How can I reach it as quickly and with as little effort as possible?
- Who has the best blueprint for this specific goal?
- If I were to perform certain key tasks every day, consistently, which ones are most likely to guarantee my success?

50

FOCUS ON SOLUTIONS

 Most people spend more time and energy going around problems than in trying to solve them.

— HENRY FORD, BUSINESS MAGNATE AND FOUNDER OF FORD MOTOR COMPANY.

Do you focus on solutions or do you dwell on problems?

Successful people are solution-oriented. Rather than looking for who's to blame or wasting energy dwelling on their problems, they focus on finding solutions.

I find it fascinating how people ruminate about their issues over and over again instead of focusing on finding solutions. Even worse, many people spend an insane amount of time worrying about issues they can't do anything about. If they were to stop for a minute and ask themselves, "What can I do about this?", they would surely spare themselves a great deal of unnecessary stress.

The message here is: *stop wasting your time focusing on problems*. Instead, dedicate your time to finding solutions. This is how you improve most of the failing areas of your life. To do so, avoid:

- Positioning yourself as a victim
- Dwelling on problems as a way to procrastinate and delay taking the necessary corrective actions, and
- Letting people around you waste your time (and theirs) by talking and talking without offering concrete solutions.

There are already enough challenges in the world around us. The world needs more solutions, not more problems. Like any other human being, you're a creative genius. Use your creativity to design innovative solutions to your problems and to the problems of others. You'll not only feel better, but you will make others feel better, too.

So, are you ready to become a problem solver and make the world a better place?

See also *Chapter 2. Take one hundred percent responsibility* and *Chapter 80. Focus on what you can control.*

* * *

Action step

Write down three to five things you're currently worrying about. Then, write down what you can do about each of them.

51

DON'T ASSUME, VERIFY

 Erroneous assumptions can be disastrous.

— PETER DRUCKER, MANAGEMENT CONSULTANT.

How often have you made an assumption that ended up being completely wrong?

Let's face it, our perception of reality is usually wildly inaccurate. This is because we have access to limited data and can only process a tiny fraction of the information around us. As a rule of thumb, the more information we can collect, the more accurate our guesses are likely to be. Conversely, the less information we have, the harder it will be to make sound decisions.

The truth is, we make assumptions all day long. Even our cornerstone beliefs are sometimes mere assumptions. For instance, we may be convinced we can't do something while we could probably do it once we've had enough practice.

Now, assumptions play an important role. They enable us to make quick decisions and help us navigate through the complexity of this world. The problem is, our assumptions are often wrong. For instance, a common assumption is to believe others think or act the same way we do. This is often not the case. We may not shop online, buy a $1,000 mobile phone or get offended easily but it doesn't mean others won't.

Why do these differences matter? Because to obtain results in the real world, you must understand reality and see it the way it is—not the way you want it to be. People can often think and act in ways that make little sense to you, and that's okay. Your role is to look at the facts and keep experimenting so that you receive valuable feedback from the reality around you. In short, you mustn't assume, you must test. For example, rather than assuming a book cover will sell just because I like it, I test it and see how the market reacts.

Making inaccurate assumptions can be more costly than you think. You might:

1. Give up on dating someone because you believe your date doesn't like you,
2. Avoid trying a new idea because you think it's stupid, or
3. Refrain from pursuing a goal because you believe it's out of your reach.

To sum up, instead of trying to read people's minds and make hasty assumptions, keep an open mind and test, test, test. This is the best way to start aligning yourself with reality and to achieve results in the long term. The person with the most accurate model of reality is usually the most effective in turning his or her goals into tangible results.

Don't guess, test. Don't assume, verify.

* * *

Action step

What are the biggest assumptions you might be making in your life right now? Write down a few of them. What are the consequences of holding onto these assumptions?

52

CULTIVATE LONG-TERM THINKING

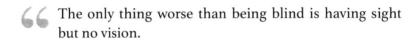 The only thing worse than being blind is having sight but no vision.

— HELLEN KELLER, AUTHOR AND POLITICAL ACTIVIST.

Do you have a long-term vision for your life?

Your ability to think long-term is one of the best predictors of success, and it starts by creating a specific vision for your life. Only when you have a clear idea of what you want your future to be like, can you identify what to focus on every day to make your vision a reality.

Sadly, most people have a fuzzy vision at best. As a result, they wander through their days, being easily distracted by shiny objects. They end up reacting to their environment, often working for other people's goals instead of pursuing their own.

Ask yourself this question: "If I keep doing what I'm doing today, will I end up where I want to be in five years?" When your answer is "no" for too many days, you know you have to make serious changes. Having a long-term vision is beneficial because it:

- Forces you to reflect on your values and goals (and cultivates self-awareness while doing so),
- Helps you identify what to focus on and what to ignore,
- Gives you a stronger sense of purpose and keeps you excited, and
- Primes your subconscious mind so that it seeks valuable information and identifies opportunities.

Having a vision also encourages you to develop a clear strategy to reach it. In turn, this drives you to create a more reliable model of reality. Remember, without a long-term vision, instead of being proactive, you will react to your external environment and people's incessant demands. You may help others achieve their goals, but you probably won't achieve yours.

Think long term and you'll achieve far better results than most people.

* * *

Action step

Where do you want to be mentally, physically and financially ten years from now? And why is that important to you?

53

SCHEDULE THINKING TIME

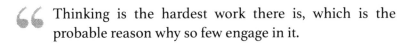 Thinking is the hardest work there is, which is the probable reason why so few engage in it.

— HENRY FORD, BUSINESS MAGNATE AND FOUNDER OF
FORD MOTOR COMPANY.

People worry, daydream, fantasize or repeat what they hear, but they seldom think for themselves. Thinking is not:

- Dwelling on the past,
- Worrying about the future,
- Seeing yourself as a victim,
- Complaining,
- Trying to validate your current beliefs (political beliefs, religious beliefs, et cetera),
- Making quick assumptions, or
- Repeating what you've heard from so-called experts.

Most people assume they think while they're simply engaging in one or several of the activities above. Your ability to think is another of your superpowers. Don't underestimate it. As you allocate time to thinking each week, you'll be able to refine your vision, boost your productivity and improve your happiness. Cultivating the habit of thinking deeply will allow you to step back and look at the bigger picture. As a result, you'll be better equipped to make better decisions (i.e., improve your model of reality). For instance, you can use your thinking time to:

- Confirm you're moving into the right direction,
- Reflect on what you could have done better,
- Optimize your processes to boost your productivity or enhance your well-being, or
- Brainstorm innovative ways to skyrocket your results in various areas of your life.

Remember, you must refine your model of reality, and it starts by taking a step back to look at the big picture and think. Accurate thinking, backed with consistent action, will help you achieve tangible results in the real world.

So, schedule at least one hour a week for thinking time. Think more and you will reap awesome benefits long term.

Action step

Schedule one hour of thinking time either today or later this week. Check whether you're moving into the right direction and brainstorm innovative ways to improve your life or to reach your goals.

54

CHALLENGE THE STATUS QUO

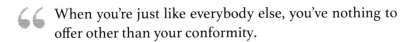 When you're just like everybody else, you've nothing to offer other than your conformity.

— Wayne Dyer, psychologist and author.

If you keep doing what everybody else is doing, you'll obtain the same results they obtain. As a reminder:

- 70% of Americans "go to work without much enthusiasm or passion" (according to a Rockport Institute survey), and
- Only 39% of Americans say they have enough savings to cover a $1,000 emergency room visit or car repair (according to the personal finance site, Bankrate).

Do you plan to become one of the people in these statistics?

If not, you must challenge your current vision of what you believe is and is not possible for you.

For instance, refute the idea that it's okay to stay at a job you hate because it's "the normal thing to do". Instead, decide what career you want to design and do everything necessary to make that career a reality.

Avoid following the herd. Instead, learn to think for yourself. Decide exactly what you want and create a clear action plan to travel from where you are to where you want to be. If you fail to decide what you want and fail to go after it pro-actively, society will decide for you. Furthermore, society often doesn't have your best interests at heart.

The key message is, don't assume things are the way they are and can't or shouldn't be changed. Instead, think. Challenge the status quo. Look for alternative paths. Find better solutions. Refuse to be a victim. Strive to become a creator. There are already enough people thinking in the same, mediocre way. Don't be one of them.

Finally, remember that society isn't an abstract thing outside of you. Society is made of real people. You, too, are part of society. As you change and act differently, you inevitably start changing society, even if it's only by a tiny amount.

You have more power than you think. So, make sure you use this power to challenge the status quo and design the life you crave.

Action step

What is one thing that most people accept but you're unwilling to do the same? What are you going to do about it?

55

ASK SMART QUESTIONS

> Quality questions create a quality life. Successful people ask better questions, and as a result, they get better answers.

— TONY ROBBINS, AUTHOR AND LIFE COACH.

- Why does it always happen to me?
- Why am I always the one who ...?
- Why is life so hard?

Do you expect any insightful answers to come out of the above questions?

The questions you ask yourself will determine your thinking. When you ask yourself better questions, you'll produce better answers and, as a result, you will take more effective action.

Here are some types of questions you want to ask yourself:

"How" questions

Often, people limit themselves wondering if they can do X, Y, Z. Rather than doing the same and doubting yourself, focus on what you could do by asking yourself "how" questions:

- How can I achieve this goal?
- How can I make more money?
- How can I design a career that I love?
- How can I find the ideal partner?
- How can I retire early?

"How" questions will force you to brainstorm ideas and find solutions. Instead of focusing on your limitations, you'll be focusing on possibilities.

Similar questions are:

- What would I need to do to...?
- What would it take for me to...?
- What could I do to...?

"Who" questions

To achieve anything in life, you'll need the help of other people. In that regard, some powerful questions are:

- Who has already achieved the goals I'm trying to achieve?
- Who has the resources I need (in terms of connections, time, money et cetera)?
- Who can help me achieve my goal faster?

"What if" questions

"What if" questions allow you to envision an ideal future without the pressure of having to make it a reality (yet). Some examples are:

- What if I could wake up every day excited to go to work?
- What if I could become the absolute best in the world in my field?
- What if I could be happy most of the time?

When it comes to "what if" questions, there is an infinite number of empowering questions you can ask yourself. Try it out.

Specific questions

The more specific the questions, the easier it is to find effective answers. This is particularly useful when trying to achieve tangible results or solve problems. Below are some examples:

- How can I double my income in the next twelve months?
- How can I lose ten pounds of excess weight in the next thirty days?
- How can I work only four days a week?

Remember, your mind will always try to answer the questions you ask yourself. Thus, ask high-quality questions. The better questions you ask, the better results you will obtain in the long term.

You can visualize the process as follows:

Better questions —> better answers —> feel better/more empowered —> take better actions —> obtain better results.

* * *

Action step

Write three of the most empowering questions you can think of. Start reflecting on them and do so for at least a few minutes.

56

TAKE CALCULATED RISKS

 Dare to take chances, lest you leave your talent buried
in the ground.

— Phil Knight, co-founder of Nike Inc.

Are you waiting for the ideal time or opportunity?

Unfortunately, perfect timing probably doesn't exist. You may never feel one hundred percent ready to write a book, create a side business or ask that attractive person out on a date. You may believe that playing it safe is the way to go. However, not taking a risk *is* risky and comes at a high cost, such as:

- The unhappiness resulting from staying in a job you hate,
- The lack of self-esteem coming from selling yourself short and not going after what you want, and
- The regrets of not having lived your life to the fullest, wondering who you could have become.

By refusing to take calculated risks, most people dramatically reduce their chances of living the life they want. For instance:

- They refuse to invest their money because it's too risky. What if I lose all my money? What if I get scammed?
- They refrain from investing in courses, books, or seminars because they are too expensive. What if I buy a course and it doesn't work for me? What if it's a scam?
- They don't try anything new because they might fail.

Now, I'm not saying you should quit your job tomorrow or do anything silly that would put your life in jeopardy, but I encourage you to take calculated risks and to think in terms of probabilities, not certainties.

Let me share four things to help you take calculated risks:

1. Calculate probabilities.

Taking calculated risks means you understand the risks and are willing to take them.

2. Assess your risk profile.

Determine how much risk you're willing to take. For instance, if you're in your early twenties, losing money from high risk/high reward investments might be okay, but if you're about to retire, it isn't.

3. Evaluate the pros and cons.

Look at the pros and cons of taking calculated risks vs. doing nothing. For instance, for me, leaving my well-paid job was risky. The cost of staying was unhappiness.

The pros of quitting my jobs were regaining my sanity and having more freedom. The cons were not having a regular paycheck (among other things).

4. Mitigate risks.

Try to reduce the risks. For instance, rather than leaving your day job tomorrow to create your business, consider starting a side business and test your ideas first.

So, what calculated risks could you take in your life right now?

Remember, not taking any risk *is* risky. You might not pay the price now, but you *will* pay it later.

Life is about managing risk, not avoiding taking any.

* * *

Action step

What risk do you feel like taking in the near future? What can you do to ensure it's a calculated risk with limited downsides but huge upsides?

57

BETTER ANTICIPATE

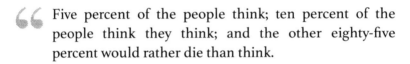 Five percent of the people think; ten percent of the people think they think; and the other eighty-five percent would rather die than think.

— THOMAS A. EDISON, INVENTOR AND BUSINESSMAN.

Would you rather prevent a disease or try to cure it after it already happened?

Your ability to think long term and anticipate problems is a critical component of your potential success. And to foresee problems effectively, you must develop an accurate model of reality which you can use to predict the future.

We often believe problems just happen. We are in no way responsible for them, right? But is that concept accurate? In truth, you could avoid many problems by projecting yourself into the future and trying to anticipate what could happen.

Here is how to become better at anticipating problems:

   1. Take an honest look at your current situation. Identify all

potential risks. Where are you slacking off? Where are you leaving room for things to worsen over time? What risks have you underestimated?

2. Ask people around you to pinpoint potential risks (having an external perspective can be very helpful).
3. Imagine some of the worst-case scenarios that could happen.
4. Think of practical ways to minimize the potential for these scenarios to occur.
5. Implement adequate countermeasures.

You are at least partially responsible for many of the problems that occur in your life. Therefore, learn to identify underlying risks and try to avoid them the best you can. Always take as much responsibility as you can for your current situation. By doing so, you'll become better at anticipating problems (see also *Chapter 2. Take one hundred percent responsibility for your life*, and *Chapter 3. Take extra responsibility*).

The point is, try to prevent, not to solve. Preventing problems will save you a lot of trouble down the road, but letting issues escalate will give you headaches.

* * *

Action step

Look at one issue you're facing right now. Then, go back to its root cause and ask yourself, "What could I have done to avoid that problem and/or limit its negative impact on my life?"

SECTION VII

GETTING THINGS DONE

If you spend too much time thinking about something, you'll never get it done.

— Bruce Lee, actor and martial artist.

True productivity isn't about being busy or working a certain number of hours per day or per week, it's about working on your most important task first and sticking to it until it's one hundred percent complete.

Unless you develop the ability to identify the right tasks (for you) and work on them diligently until you complete them, you're unlikely to become a productive person and achieve your most important goals in the long term.

Remember, your productivity is your ability to produce. Thus, whenever you work on something, ask yourself, "What exactly am I trying to produce here? What does the end result need to look like? And why does it matter?"

In this section, we'll discuss key principles that will allow you to skyrocket your productivity and become a truly effective person. Let's get started.

58

SET DAILY GOALS

 As long as you are alive, you'll either live to accomplish your own goals and dreams, or you'll be used as a resource to accomplish someone else's goals and dreams.

— GRANT CARDONE, AUTHOR AND MOTIVATIONAL
SPEAKER.

Do you have clear written goals you're working toward every day?

If you don't have goals, you risk spending your life working for someone who does. Therefore, it's vital you identify specific long-term goals and set daily goals to ensure you make progress toward them.

Daily goal setting is one of the most powerful habits for success. It will dramatically increase your productivity, allowing you to accomplish far more than you think possible in the long run. Remember this simple fact: if what you do every day doesn't move you closer to your goals, then it moves you away from them. So, ask yourself, is what you do today moving you closer to your ideal life?

To set daily goals, there is no real need to implement complicated productivity systems. Start by determining your long-term vision. Then break it down into small, manageable tasks by setting yearly goals, ninety-day goals, monthly goals, weekly goals and, finally, daily goals.

To identify the correct and essential goals, ask yourself, "What do I need to do this year (month, week, et cetera.), to achieve my long-term goals?" For me, one daily goal is usually to write a chapter of a book or a certain number of words. Your goal might be more complicated than mine, but you can always break it down into manageable tasks you can start working on today.

Then, to set your daily goals, ask yourself, "If I were to do one specific thing today, which one would allow me to make the most progress toward my goals?", and keep asking yourself this question until you have three to five tasks. Complete the first task before moving on to the next one. Repeat the process.

* * *

Action step

- Identify three to five tasks that you will work on today (make sure they move you closer to your long-term vision).
- Complete the first task before moving on to other tasks.
- Repeat this process until you complete all your tasks.

Bonus tip: an effective way to ensure you work on your most valuable task every day is to make it part of your morning ritual (see also *Chapter 21. Create a morning ritual*).

To learn in more detail how to set and achieve exciting goals, refer to my book *Goal Setting: The Ultimate Guide to Achieving Goals that Truly Excite You.*

59

FINISH WHAT YOU START

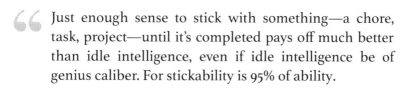 Just enough sense to stick with something—a chore, task, project—until it's completed pays off much better than idle intelligence, even if idle intelligence be of genius caliber. For stickability is 95% of ability.

— DAVID J. SCHWARTZ, UNIVERSITY PROFESSOR AND WRITER.

Do you keep jumping from one thing to the next without completing much?

If so, it might be time to start completing what you begin. "Finish starting and start finishing", as one of my friends was often told by his boss.

The problem with allowing yourself to start things without finishing them is that it soon becomes a habit. This habit not only leads to poor performance, but it also erodes your self-esteem. After all, how are you to ever going to achieve your biggest dreams if you're unable to complete smaller tasks, and complete them consistently?

As you learn to complete tasks consistently and repeatedly, you will dramatically increase your self-discipline, and you will develop more and more self-confidence. As a result, you'll be able to tackle bigger and bigger projects.

Your stickability—your ability to stick to a task or project until it is complete—will turn you into a high performer. If you were to finish just one extra task every day, just imagine how much would it impact your long-term productivity.

Everybody can start one project after another, but very few people can complete everything they start. If you find yourself with too many projects, check whether all these projects are truly urgent. Look at each one and ask yourself what would happen if you postponed this project by a month, three months, or six months? If your answer is nothing (or not much), consider delaying this specific project.

What you want to do is reduce the number of projects on your plate and fully complete the ones remaining before moving on to new projects. This start/complete cycle will skyrocket your productivity while boosting your self-confidence.

Remember, it's more important to complete a few key projects extraordinary well than to have many projects on your plate and leave half of them unfinished. You don't have an unlimited amount of energy. Use the energy you have wisely.

Action step

Do one of the two things below:

1. Write down three simple tasks and complete them today. Repeat this process for seven days.
2. Complete a task you've been procrastinating on for a while and complete it one hundred percent.

60

THINK LESS, DO MORE

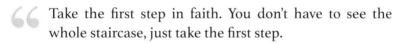 Take the first step in faith. You don't have to see the whole staircase, just take the first step.

— DR. MARTIN LUTHER KING JR., MINISTER AND ACTIVIST.

Earlier, I told you about the importance of thinking. Now, I'm telling you to think less and do more. You might be asking, what's wrong with this guy?

Yes, you do need to carve out time to think every week but, during the rest of your week, you must focus on getting things done. Most people overthink things, trying to come up with the perfect plan—or so they tell themselves. They always have good excuses for saying why "now" is not a proper time to get started. They need to do more research, build more confidence or wait for the right moment.

As previously mentioned, I'm part of a Toastmasters club, a place where people meet to practice public speaking and improve their leadership skills. One of the club members waited for months to give his first speech. He needed more time because he wanted to make sure his first speech would be "perfect".

Guess what? When he finally made his first speech, it wasn't very good. And this is exactly how it was supposed to be. Before anyone can hope to become a decent public speaker, they will need to deliver dozens, if not hundreds, of speeches. Expecting to be good the first time is unrealistic. Another example would be someone who spends years writing their first book, hoping it will be a masterpiece. This success rarely happens.

The most effective way to learn a skill is by doing it—and by doing it over and over again. We learn through repetition. Every master is a master of repetition, whether they are an outstanding writer, a martial arts expert or an accomplished public speaker. There is no exception to this rule (see also *Chapter 69. Be a master, not a dabbler*).

So, stop thinking. Stop pondering and over-planning. Instead of being a spectator, enter the arena and get your hands dirty. High achievers take action. They don't talk about how, one day, they will do something. They actually do it, and they do it right away.

Understand that there will never be a perfect time for you to work on your biggest goals and dreams. If you don't start working on them right now, you probably won't start working on them any time soon. So, think less and do more. Let go of your unrealistic expectations and get started. Yes, it will probably be a little messy at first, but that's the way it's supposed to be. Reality will sometimes give you harsh feedback. Learn from it and improve as a result. If you can do this, you will become unstoppable.

So, what are you waiting for?

* * *

Action step

Identify one thing you've been procrastinating on due to fear. Then, take that first step you've been avoiding for far too long.

61

LEVERAGE THE 80/20 PRINCIPLE

 It's not enough to be busy, so are the ants.

— HENRY DAVID THOREAU, POET AND PHILOSOPHER.

Do you have too much on your plate? Are you overwhelmed?

If so, why not apply the Pareto rule (a.k.a. The 80/20 Principle)? Although you might already be familiar with this concept, the key question is: are you applying it *consistently* every day?

The 80/20 Principle states that 80% of your results will come from 20% of your effort. Therefore, you need to identify the 20% of your effort that leads to the majority of your results.

To skyrocket your productivity, you must identify your priorities and focus on these priorities the vast majority of the time. Many people waste countless hours focusing on low-value tasks, making little or no progress toward their goals. They may do so as a way to procrastinate and avoid doing the hard work, or they may fail to realize they're focusing on the wrong tasks.

The first step to using The 80/20 Principle is to identify the few tasks that bring most of your results. For instance, for me, it's writing more books and running CPC ads. It's not posting inspirational quotes on Facebook, shooting YouTube videos, tweeting, going to conferences, or doing podcast interviews.

Here is a great question to ask yourself, "If I keep doing what I'm doing today, will I complete the project I'm working on? If so, will I achieve it as quickly and effectively as possible?"

If the answer is no, then, ask yourself what you could do differently to improve your productivity.

The 80/20 Principle is one of the most powerful tools to help you achieve any goal, and it can work in various areas of your life. Below are some questions to consider:

- Of your clients, who are the 20% that bring in 80% of your profit?
- Of your friends, who are the 20% that generate 80% of your fulfillment?
- Of your daily tasks, which 20% contribute to 80% of your well-being?
- Of your negative thoughts, which 20% create 80% of your worries?

Your time is one of your most precious resources. The purpose of The 80/20 Principle is to help you focus on what truly makes a difference when it comes to achieving success and happiness. So, use that principle as often as possible in your life and start regaining your sanity.

* * *

Action step

Select one area of your life. Using your action guide, create an exhaustive list of all the actions you're currently taking. Then, answer the question below:

Of these actions, which 20% lead to 80% of your results in this specific area?

Circle one to three key actions that you believe are the most effective. These are the tasks you want to focus on. A good idea is to make them part of your morning ritual (See *Chapter 21. Create a morning ritual*).

62

MAXIMIZE YOUR SPEED OF IMPLEMENTATION

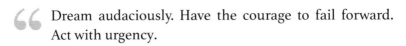 Dream audaciously. Have the courage to fail forward. Act with urgency.

— PHIL KNIGHT, CO-FOUNDER OF NIKE INC.

Many people talk about how, one day, they will open a restaurant, create a side business or write a book. However, this "one day" never seems to arrive.

Successful people are not interested in daydreaming. They are committed to making their goals a reality. To do so, they train themselves to be pro-active, moving toward the achievement of any projects they're excited about. Because they understand their time is limited, they continuously attempt to maximize their speed of implementation. They ask themselves, "How can I work toward this goal right now?" Or "What do I need to do to complete this project as quickly and efficiently as possible?"

More generally, successful people are action-oriented. They endeavor to implement what they learn immediately. If a trusted person recommends a book, they buy it on the spot and might even read it the same day. In short, they have a strong sense of urgency which allows them to build momentum and accomplish far more than the average person ever will.

You are *not* going to live forever. Your time on this planet is limited. Therefore, cultivate the habit of taking immediate action. Otherwise, you'll probably never achieve your biggest goals and dreams. A good way to put it is: *Be impatient short term, but patient long term.* Most people do the exact opposite. They tell themselves it's okay to postpone today's actions, but they still want immediate results (despite taking little or no action toward them).

No! This is wrong!

Set deadlines and create urgency. Aim to complete short-term projects quickly and effectively. Then, repeat the process over a long period of time until you achieve your biggest goals. This, and only this, will allow you to succeed.

The bottom line is, aim to increase your speed of implementation and demand more of yourself. Practice working faster and better. You can do better work and you can probably do it faster, too.

* * *

Action step

Select one exciting goal. Imagine you were given a power called, "Extreme speed of implementation". What can you do right now to make progress toward your main goal?

63

GET STARTED

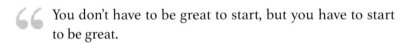 You don't have to be great to start, but you have to start to be great.

— ZIG ZIGLAR, SALESMAN AND MOTIVATIONAL SPEAKER.

Consider one thing you've been wanting to do for a while but haven't started yet. What excuses are you telling yourself to explain your inability to start?

You can spend hours brainstorming and create an incredibly detailed action plan. However, real clarity will only come when you start. There is no real need to identify exactly how you're going to achieve your goals. Reality will give you the necessary feedback. Furthermore, setbacks will test your motivation and give you the chance to refine your vision and strengthen your "why".

But all these things will only come once you start. You can't stay on the bench watching others living the life you want. You can't be an extra in the movie of your life. This is a sure way to keep your true potential buried. You must be in the arena, not in the bleachers. And, for now, all it requires is for you to take the first step.

So, what one action could you take today to start moving toward the goal you've been putting off for way too long? Is it to send an email, register for a course, or buy a book? You only need to know the first step, then the second step will be revealed to you in due course. You have to trust the process. Sure, brainstorm, plan and do your best to come up with an effective blueprint (see also *Chapter 48. Look for role models* and *Chapter 49. Try to dramatically reduce your learning curve*). But, most importantly, get started! You can always refine your plan over time.

Take the first step and begin the process of alignment with reality. Learn from your setbacks. Refine your plan. Clarify your vision. Upgrade your skills. Then, watch yourself achieving things you didn't believe possible.

* * *

Action step

Using your action guide, write down your first step. This first step could be toward the achievement of any sort of goals in any area of your life. That's up to you. Here are my recommendations:

- Look at one activity you've been thinking of starting for a while.
- Identify what the first step would be for you.
- Take that first step today or later this week and see where it takes you.

64

FOCUS ON THE PROCESS

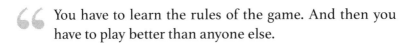 You have to learn the rules of the game. And then you
have to play better than anyone else.

— ALBERT EINSTEIN, PHYSICIST AND NOBEL PRIZE WINNER.

Success is a process, not an outcome.

Instead of focusing on the result, focus on the process you're going through every day. It's easy to become discouraged when your expectations are crushed over and over again (and they will be), but what really matters the most is that you stick to the daily process and keep refining it over time. With the right process, you'll likely achieve your goals, no matter how ambitious they may be.

Now, whatever your vision, you need to have both process goals and result goals.

Process goals are the goals you have control over. It's up to you whether you reach them or not. Some examples would be:

- Writing five books this year,
- Running for fifteen minutes every day, or

- Going on a date with your partner one evening a week.

Result goals are targets you want to reach. Whether you achieve these goals is only partially within your control. Some examples are:

- Making $80,000 this year,
- Selling 50,000 books, or
- Losing thirty pounds in excess weight.

Both types of goals are important. Result goals give you a clear direction, and process goals determine what you need to do to maximize the chances you hit your target (i.e., your result goals).

You must cherish your process goals. You must stick to the process and remain consistent week after week, month after month, year after year. This is how you will dramatically increase your chances of achieving your results goals. You must learn to remain emotionally resilient and keep going despite all the challenges you'll face. The world around you may be collapsing, yet you must hang in on, refining your process and becoming better along the way (see *Section IX. Developing emotional resilience*).

Once you have set your target (result goals), focus on the process. Immerse yourself in it. What you do every day, consistently, will get you there. Successful people learn to enjoy the process. Be one of them. Learn to love the process and you will most certainly achieve your goals.

* * *

Action step

Write down one goal you want to achieve (a result goal). Then, write down the process goals that will most likely lead you to achieve that goal.

65

THINK PROJECTS NOT TASKS

> ❝ Efficiency is doing things right; effectiveness is doing the right things.

> — PETER DRUCKER, MANAGEMENT CONSULTANT.

To maximize your productivity, you must keep the big picture in mind at all times. You have to know why you're doing what you're doing. Otherwise, you'll keep working on useless tasks that don't move you closer to your goals.

This is why you must cultivate the habit of thinking in terms of projects not just tasks. Don't just focus on completing individual tasks efficiently. Instead, focus on finishing whole projects as effectively as possible. There is nothing worse than working on tasks that didn't need to be done in the first place.

True productivity comes from completing projects one by one consistently. When you are part of a large organization, it's easy to lose sight of the bigger picture. As a result, you may end up spending most of your time working on tasks without even knowing why. To a certain extent, this might be inevitable. However, you want to keep training yourself to think in terms of overall projects. To do so, practice asking yourself smart questions that will boost your productivity. Below are some examples:

- What exactly am I trying to achieve here? What does the end result look like?
- What is the fastest way to complete this project? Who can help me? What case studies are out there?
- What's the best approach?
- What should I avoid doing to stop wasting time?

Clearly define your projects, limit their numbers, then start working on the tasks that matter. Each morning, remind yourself of what exactly you're trying to accomplish that day. Make sure that each task you focus on aligns with the project you are trying to complete.

Think in terms of projects. Keep completing major projects and you'll see that your results will improve (read also *Chapter 59. Finish what you start* and *Chapter 61. Leverage the 80/20 principle*).

* * *

Action step

Reflect on the tasks you've been working on in the past seven days. Now, think of the few key projects you're trying to complete. Are these the most important tasks you should be focusing on to complete these projects? If not, what could you be doing differently?

66

FOCUS ON ONE THING AT A TIME

 To do two things at once is to do neither.

— PUBLILIUS SYRUS, LATIN WRITER.

Your true power comes from your ability to focus your limited energy on one specific thing, and one thing only. Focus is your ultimate power. Successful people are extremely focused. They value their time—and what they do with it—above anything else. Average people scatter their focus. A poor focus will destroy your potential, kill your peace of mind, and ensure you never reach the level of success you're aspiring for.

Achieving any major goal requires tons of energy. When you scatter your energy amongst too many projects, you generate a huge amount of friction. Over time, this waste of energy accumulates, and severely limits how much you can achieve. This is why it's usually better to focus on one major goal or project at a time until it is attained.

For instance, let's say you want to complete three important projects that you estimate will each take three months. You could work on all of them at the same time for nine months or you could work on one project at a time and complete it before moving on to the next one.

The second option is often much more effective. When you focus most of your time and energy on one thing, you become far more productive while avoiding the risk of being overwhelmed. You'll likely finish each of your projects faster that way.

Note that it will also depend on the nature of your project, but whenever you can, aim to focus most of your energy on one specific task at a time until you have completed each one. Then move on to the next one.

* * *

Action step

Using your action guide, make a list of all the major projects you're currently working on. Then, ask yourself the following question: if I could only focus on one thing, what would that thing be?

To identify your one thing, consider the following:

- How much impact working on that one thing would have on your life overall.
- How well it aligns with your definition of success (i.e., is it moving you toward what you really want? Does it align with your core values?).
- How much excitement it generates.

Once you have identified your one thing, ask yourself how you could allocate time during the day to focus single-mindedly on it. I recommend you make it part of your morning ritual whenever possible.

67

ELIMINATE DISTRACTIONS AND BOOST YOUR FOCUS

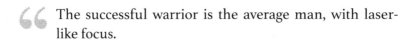 The successful warrior is the average man, with laser-like focus.

— BRUCE LEE, ACTOR AND MARTIAL ARTIST.

How often do you check your emails? How much time do you spend on social media?

In today's world, distractions are everywhere. One study showed that, on average, office workers check their emails seventy-four times per day. Another study conducted by Gloria Mark, a researcher at the University of California, revealed that, *"each employee spent only eleven minutes on any given project before being interrupted."* Under these conditions, it's no wonder the average worker struggles to be productive.

To boost your focus and enhance your productivity, you must learn to eliminate distractions while reducing interruptions as much as possible.

To simplify, we can divide distractions into two categories: internal distractions and external distractions.

Internal distractions represent your thoughts and state of flow. Are you one hundred percent focused on the task at hand, or is your mind continuously wandering? For many of us, our minds are often restless. According to research conducted by Harvard psychologists, Matthew Killingsworth and Daniel Gilbert, people spend as much as 46.9% of their waking hours thinking about something other than what they're doing.

To reduce internal distractions, you need to become mindful of your thoughts. Whenever you notice that your mind starts to wander, refocus on the task. Keep doing this over and over. To sharpen your focus, work on one task single-mindedly for 45 to 60 minutes before taking a break (see also *Chapter 71. Take effective breaks*).

External distractions represent interruptions by other people. Studies have shown that, once distracted, a worker needs twenty-five minutes to get into the state of flow he or she was in before the interruption. Therefore, to maintain a high level of focus, limit interruptions as much as possible. For instance, ask your colleagues not to disturb you during certain times of the day. Turn off your phone (if you can). Alternatively, talk to your supervisor to find a workable solution.

The longer you can work without being interrupted (while taking effective breaks), the more productive you will become—and the better you'll feel about yourself.

Still not convinced?

Researchers at the Institute of Psychiatry at the University of London found that workers distracted by phone calls, emails and text messages saw a decrease in IQ greater than smoking pot or losing a night's sleep (the average IQ was reduced by 10 points).

So, work on eliminating distractions and your productivity will significantly increase.

To learn in more depth how to develop laser-sharp focus and eliminate distractions, you can refer to the third book in the Mastery

Series, *Master Your Focus: A Practical Guide to Stop Chasing the Next Thing and Focus on What Matters Until It's Done.*

* * *

Action step

Today, practice working on one task for forty-five minutes without interruption. Whenever you catch your mind wandering, bring your attention back to the task at hand.

68

GO TEMPORARILY OUT OF BALANCE

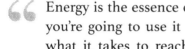 Energy is the essence of life. Every day you decide how you're going to use it by knowing what you want and what it takes to reach that goal, and by maintaining focus.

— OPRAH WINFREY, TALK SHOW HOST AND TELEVISION PRODUCER.

Do you have too many issues to solve or goals to achieve?

We all have many issues we would like to solve or dreams we would like to achieve. However, the energy we have available each day is limited. As we discussed previously, your ability to focus is key, since it prevents you from wasting energy by jumping from one thing to the next. The same principle applies here.

To achieve outstanding results in all areas of your life, you must temporarily go out of balance. Think about it this way: imagine you're broke, out of shape, single and jobless. Do you think you have enough time, energy, and willpower to make money, get back in shape, find your ideal partner and design a fulfilling career all at once? While you could certainly work on all these goals at the same time, you'll only get mediocre results at best. Instead, I encourage you to attack the one area of your life that would make the biggest difference.

So, if you were to focus most of your time and effort in improving one single area, which one would have the biggest positive impact on your life?

For instance, if you hate your job, perhaps your main focus in the coming months should be to find a better job. However, if you're unhealthy, you probably want to take care of your health first.

The point is, choose one major area you want to get serious results in. Then, commit to spending at least 80% of your time/effort improving that area until you attain the tangible results you're looking for. Then, and only then, move on to the next area you want to improve.

Go out of balance and improve your life one area at a time. This is often the most effective way to design your ideal life in the long term. If you don't apply enough pressure, you won't be able to build the momentum needed to have breakthroughs in various areas of your life.

So, what one area are you going to focus on in the coming weeks/months?

* * *

Action step

If you decided to focus most of your time and effort on one area right now, which one would have the biggest positive impact on your life?

69

BE A MASTER, NOT A DABBLER

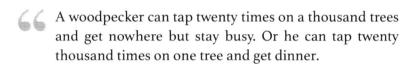 A woodpecker can tap twenty times on a thousand trees and get nowhere but stay busy. Or he can tap twenty thousand times on one tree and get dinner.

— SETH GODIN, AUTHOR AND ENTREPRENEUR.

Do you have a track record of giving up before obtaining results? Do you start one course after the next, never getting anywhere?

If so, you likely suffer from the "Shiny Object Syndrome". To overcome that syndrome you need to develop a "mastery mindset".

People who fail to go deep with whatever skill they try to learn will never achieve anything significant. To reach any of your major goals, you must develop a mastery mindset. Having a mastery mindset means you approach any goal with the firm commitment to follow through to the end. You will practice over and over until you get the desired result. Sadly, many people set goals but aren't committed to achieving them. They might attend a course and try implementing a few things, but they never delve deeply enough to master anything. These people are "dabblers". They dabble with their side hustle, they experiment with countless diets, or they start project after project, never completing any of them. If you recognize yourself in the above description, realize that you will *never* achieve any of your greatest goals if you keep behaving that way.

On the other side of the spectrum are the masters. Masters are obsessed with repetition and are determined to delve as deep as they can with everything they learn. To do so, they practice over and over again. They know that if other people can attain desired results, they will too—as long as they keep practicing.

You, too, must become a master. You must decide that, to reach whatever goals that matter to you, you will keep practicing, experimenting, tweaking, refining, and fine-tuning until you achieve tangible results. Masters don't complain because things don't work; they find a way to make them work, and so should you.

Below are some key characteristics of masters:

- They're firmly committed to reaching their goals,
- They embrace repetition and enjoy the process leading to the achievement of their goals,
- They apply everything they learn until they excel at their chosen skill/field of study,
- They're humble, willing to learn and question their approach whenever needed, and
- They think long term and remain patient, knowing that things often take longer than expected.

To achieve exceptional results, get rid of your dabbling mentality and become a master. Stop knowing things only intellectually. Avoid remaining superficial. Instead, delve as deep as you can and keep practicing. This simple shift alone will change everything for you.

* * *

Action step

- Think of one goal you failed to achieve in the past.

- Now, imagine how things would have been different if you had a mastery mindset.
- Write down a few things you would have done differently.
- Then, select one of your major goals and imagine what working on it with a mastery mindset would look like.

70

FALL IN LOVE WITH CONSISTENCY

 Long-term consistency trumps short-term intensity.

— BRUCE LEE, ACTOR AND MARTIAL ARTIST.

It's what you do every single day that transforms your life, not what you do every other day.

Consistency is one of the major keys to success. It is what turns average people into superheroes. Imagine if you could stick to a couple of habits every single day for the next six months? Twelve months? Five years? Ten years? How much momentum would this create in your life, and how much more productive would you become?

For example, imagine if you were to work on your most important task first thing in the morning every single day? What would this do to your productivity? Wouldn't most of your biggest goals and dreams become your reality?

The truth is, you're only a couple of habits away from dramatically improving your results in many areas of your life. Now, let me share with you eight of the most powerful habits you can adopt:

1. **Working on your most important tasks first thing in the morning.** Creating a habit of tackling your key tasks early in the morning will ensure you complete the most important thing every single day. This simple habit alone can supercharge your productivity.

2. **Reading your goals.** Reviewing your written goals every day will boost your productivity and ensure you continue to move in the right direction.

3. **Setting daily goals.** By setting goals every day, you'll end up in a far different (and better) place in a few years from now than you otherwise would.

4. **Meditating.** Among other benefits, adopting a daily meditation routine will boost your focus, enhance your happiness, and reduce stress.

5. **Practicing gratitude.** Starting your day by expressing gratitude for all the wonderful things you have going for you will also boost your mood.

6. **Exercising.** Doing some kind of exercise daily will enhance your mood, improve your health, and increase your productivity.

7. **Consuming inspirational materials.** Starting your day by reading or listening to inspirational or educational content will turn you into a full-blown optimist.

8. **Self-reflecting.** Spending some time every evening to reflect on what happened earlier that day will allow you to cultivate more self-awareness. Good questions to ask yourself are: "What did I do well today?", "What could I have done even better?", and "What will I do differently tomorrow?"

Most successful people have daily routines that help them feel good and perform at their best. Create your own daily routine and start building more consistency in your life. This will impact your life in more ways you may imagine (see also *Chapter 21. Create a morning ritual*).

So, what daily habit(s) will you implement starting today?

* * *

Action step

Select one daily habit and commit to sticking to it for the next thirty days in a row.

71

TAKE EFFECTIVE BREAKS

 He that can take rest is greater than he that can take cities.

— BENJAMIN FRANKLIN, WRITER, INVENTOR AND POLITICIAN.

You have to make every single minute of your day count, right? So, skip lunch, avoid taking coffee breaks and keep hustling until your eyes bleed. This is how you will skyrocket your productivity for sure.

Or is it?

First, as we mentioned before, you need to make sure you're doing the right things and not just doing things right (see *Chapter 61. Leverage the 80/20 Principle*).

But you also need to be very intentional in the way you work and rest. As the best-selling writer and high-performance coach, Brendon Burchard, showed in *High Performance Habits*, high performers take regular breaks. They don't work eight or ten hours in a row without resting.

Many people believe that if they work longer hours, take fewer breaks and avoid "wasting time", they will boost their productivity. However, this is not how your brain works. Yes, time is valuable, but the energy level you bring into any task is even more important. If you fail to take breaks, your ability to focus will decrease dramatically. Consequently, you must learn to manage both your time *and* your energy smartly.

The key is to be intentional in how you use your time. It means planning your year, month, week and day. It means knowing at any given moment why you're doing what you're doing. It also means being intentional with the way you take breaks. For instance, you might decide to take a five- to ten-minute break every forty-five minutes.

Now, you might think that it's crazy.

"If I take ten minutes every forty-five minutes, that's almost ninety minutes wasted every day."

But that's only because you think in terms of time spent instead of your energy levels and your intentionality (i.e., what you're trying to accomplish).

A person who works in forty-five-minute blocks and who knows exactly what he or she needs to accomplish will usually be more productive—and often significantly more so—than a person who works eight hours straight without breaks.

Below are some example of time blocks you can experiment with:

Every seventy-five to ninety minutes: Robert Pozen, author of *Extreme Productivity: Boost Your Results, Reduce Your Hours*, recommends taking a break every seventy-five to ninety minutes.

Every fifty-two minutes: The startup, Draugiem Group, found that the most productive people took frequent breaks, working fifty-two minutes and taking seventeen-minute rests.

Every twenty-five minutes (Pomodoro technique): The Pomodoro technique entails working twenty-five minutes and taking five-minute breaks.

I understand that, as an employee, you might not be able to take that many breaks. If so, try to take short breaks. It could be as simple as standing up for one to two minutes or doing breathing exercises.

Learn to work in blocks and take regular breaks between the blocks. Then, see what happens to your productivity (see also *Chapter 17. Be intentional during your day*).

* * *

Action step

Experiment with each of the time-blocks above for a week. Then, select the one that works best for you.

SECTION VIII

MAINTAINING AN OPEN MIND

An open mind leaves a chance for someone to drop a worthwhile thought in it.

— MARK TWAIN, WRITER AND HUMORIST.

Successful people are continually learning. They don't consider their education complete once they graduate from university. Instead, they see graduation as the beginning of a new learning experience that will last until the day they die.

Being willing to humble yourself and keep learning no matter how much you already know is a characteristic shared by most successful people. One key reason being open-minded is so important is that it will allow you to learn more and learn faster. As a result, you'll be able to keep refining your model of reality as opposed to assuming you already know it all.

In this section, we'll see what you can do to remain a perpetual student of life and achieve higher levels of success throughout your life.

72

LEVERAGE YOUR CURIOSITY

 I have no special talent. I am just passionately curious.

— ALBERT EINSTEIN, PHYSICIST AND NOBLE PRIZE WINNER.

What are you curious about? What do you want to learn more about?

Curiosity is another of your superpowers. Thus, I invite you to pay more attention to the things you're curious about. What fields are you interested in? What topics of conversation get you excited? During your spare time, what are you naturally drawn toward? Whatever topics pique your interest, dive deeper into them.

Being curious will enable you to refine your model of reality and improve your understanding of the way things work. It will also allow you to keep learning and persevering when the going gets tough. Passionate people don't give up that easily, do they?

Curious people never assume they know everything. Instead, they try to deepen their understanding. Since they crave more knowledge, they learn faster than anybody else. With their insatiable desire for information, they read more and study more, sustaining a high level of excitement over the long term. They don't merely focus on the end goal. They also enjoy the process, and this makes them more likely to keep going, no matter how tough it may be.

Don't overestimate the power of curiosity. Take time to identify all the things you're interested in. Then, seek ways to become even more curious about these things. What more could you learn? What have you been overlooking? What are the highest performers in your field doing that you're not doing yet? Don't you want to know?

Keep asking questions. Keep learning. When you *truly* want to know everything there is to know, you'll eventually become one of the most knowledgeable people in your field. This is inevitable. So, stay curious and look for answers to all your questions. Do this, and you'll find answers to most of them.

* * *

Action step

What is the one thing you're the most curious about? Go learn more about that thing by reading articles online, buying a book, or taking a course.

73

EMBRACE FLEXIBILITY

 Nothing is softer or more flexible than water, yet nothing can resist it.

— LAO TZU, ANCIENT CHINESE PHILOSOPHER.

Life is unpredictable and ever-changing. As such, circumstances will change over time. Perhaps, your exciting goal is now out of your reach. Or perhaps, it has become irrelevant and doesn't mean anything to you anymore.

While being persistent is important, there are times where you must be flexible enough to change your goals, reframe them and, in some cases, give up on them. In the end, the purpose of your goals is not only to improve your future but also your present. Sticking to a goal that is not enjoyable and unlikely to boost your future happiness is a sign of proverbial insanity.

We often believe that once we've achieved a specific goal it will make us happy. However, this is seldom, if ever, the case. For instance, becoming wealthy or famous won't solve all your problems, nor will it enhance your level of fulfillment overnight. Whatever goal you're working on, you must ensure that:

1. You enjoy working on it (for the most part), and
2. It will allow you to design the future you genuinely want.

If you struggle to make progress on your goal or if it doesn't excite you anymore, it might be time to change it. But before you do that, make sure you're dumping it for the right reasons. To do so, answer the following question: "Do I want to give up on that goal because I'm scared or tired, or is it because it's not what I want anymore?"

Giving up on a goal because it's out of alignment with your biggest vision is fine, but doing so because you're scared, you lack confidence or you are unwilling to do the work isn't. This is when you want to be honest with yourself.

You don't want to continually give up on one goal after the next. This behavior won't allow you to get very far in life. My advice here is to be flexible enough to change your goals when they don't align with your bigger vision but avoid giving up on them as a way to avoid fear or discomfort.

* * *

Action step

Select a major goal you're working on right now. Then, ask yourself the following questions:

- Do I enjoy working on this goal?
- Does it help me design the future I want?

74

NEVER STOP LEARNING

 If you leave your growth to randomness, you'll always live in the land of mediocrity.

— Brendon Burchard, author and high-performance coach.

Your ability to learn is one of your biggest gifts. To paraphrase the business philosopher, Jim Rohn, traditional education will get you a job, but self-education will make you a fortune.

Success is a process you must stick to every day, and so is learning. You cannot stop learning and expect to stay at the top of your game for the rest of your career. You must continually learn and upgrade your skills. Successful people are learners. They study courses, read books or attend seminars. They understand that the more information they accumulate, the better and more accurate the decisions they are able to make.

Thus, you must cultivate the habit of reading every single day. By reading for fifteen minutes a day, you will be able to read ten to twenty books a year. Alternatively, you can use your commuting time to listen to audiobooks.

You may lose your job or all your money, but nobody can ever take away the skills and knowledge you've acquired. Learning and developing new skills is the best way to ensure that you will always be in demand. So, aim to become the type of person who can find a job or create ventures in almost any situation. In short, self-education is your best insurance policy. And, thanks to the internet, in today's world you have access to an almost unlimited amount of information. You have no excuse not to learn any of the skills you need to achieve your goals.

In conclusion, in a world changing at a faster pace than ever before, you must be able to adapt and learn new skills as quickly and effectively as possible. If you can do this, you won't have to worry excessively about finding a job and paying the bills. But if you fail to educate yourself, sooner or later you are likely to pay the price. Educating yourself is your responsibility. Don't expect society, your company or even the school system to do it for you. Never stop learning (see also *Chapter 69. Be a master, not a dabbler*).

* * *

Action step

Develop the habit of reading or listening to educational content for fifteen minutes every day.

75

STAY HUMBLE

 I'm always asked, 'What's the secret to success?' But there are no secrets. Be humble. Stay hungry. And always be the hardest worker in the room.

— DWAYNE JOHNSON, ACTOR AND PROFESSIONAL
WRESTLER.

Your ability to remain humble and learn from the people around you is vital. We sometimes believe we know more than others and are unwilling to take their opinion into consideration. Also, we can sometimes be afraid of looking bad if we don't have all the answers.

Here is the truth: you don't need all the answers. Neither is this possible. Always be willing to listen to others. You don't have to agree with them or take their advice, but you should be open-minded enough to listen to what they have to say. Sometimes, the people who know nothing about your goals or your business can come up with the best ideas.

Also, we all have biases that cloud our judgment. Staying humble and being open to feedback will allow you to make better decisions and further refine your model of reality, thereby reducing your blind spots. Listening to other people is an effective way to receive feedback from the reality around you. It will help you answer questions such as, "What am I doing well?", "What could I be doing better?", or "What am I overlooking?"

Now, saying "I don't know" and accepting feedback is one of the hardest things to do. Many people would rather be in denial, especially when their current reality is not what they want. However, refusing to face reality will not allow you to achieve your goals. It will only keep your flawed model of reality alive.

Therefore, humble yourself. Realize you don't know everything and be willing to learn, whether this is by actively seeking feedback from people around you, reading books or gathering relevant information.

If you refuse to question yourself and what you do, you'll not only slow down your growth, you'll also be a pain in the neck to work with. Nobody wants to be around someone who is always "right". So, stay humble and remain open to learning.

*　*　*

Action step

In what ways are you not as humble as you could be? Write down some of your answers. What one specific thing could you do to change that?

76

MAKE THE MOST OF YOUR MISTAKES

 In the real world, the smartest people are people who make mistakes and learn. In school, the smartest people don't make mistakes.

— ROBERT T. KIYOSAKI, BUSINESSMAN AND AUTHOR.

Your ability to learn from every single one of your mistakes will allow you to grow faster and achieve better results than most people.

Sadly, we often fail to learn from our mistakes. This is usually because we're afraid to face reality. We don't want to accept the idea that we may not be as smart or talented as we would like to be. As a result, instead of analyzing what we did wrong and correcting our course, we sweep our mistakes under the rug and move on. Paradoxically, this inability to confront reality actually prevents us from developing our talent and skills. However, you need to understand this:

Denial of reality leads to mediocrity.

You can't improve unless you acknowledge your mistakes and shortcomings. To grow, you must align yourself with reality. You do this by becoming more self-aware and being willing to correct your course of action based on repeated feedback from reality—mistakes, comments, advice from people around you, et cetera.

So, what mistakes are you repeating? What harsh realities are you unwilling to face right now? It might be time for you to get real here. Ignoring reality will prevent you from making the best use of your talents and achieving the success and happiness you deserve.

Making mistakes is not a problem and is, to some extent, inevitable. In fact, if you're not failing, you're probably not trying anything new. The only real error is failing to learn from your mistakes.

The bottom line is, be willing to learn from every single one of your mistakes and never stop improving. If you can do that, you'll grow far beyond anything you think is currently possible.

* * *

Action step

Learn from your mistakes by asking yourself the following questions:

- What failures am I refusing to face head-on and learn from?
- What mistakes may I be making right now or in the near future?
- What could I do about it?

77

LET GO OF YOUR EGO

 Pride is pleasure arising from a man's thinking too highly of himself.

— Baruch Spinoza, philosopher.

Have you ever watched the show, *The Profit*?

In this fascinating show, serial entrepreneur, Marcus Lemonis, helps struggling businesses, by offering his own money in exchange for an equity share of their companies.

What surprised me the most in the show was how defensive many of the owners were. Their behavior and attitude seemed to be the main reason they were struggling. Often, they were:

- Unwilling to reconsider the way they do business and let go of things that clearly didn't work,
- Unwilling to take responsibility for their poor results (instead, they blamed employees, customers, suppliers, or external circumstances),
- Unable to let go of control and allow employees to do their job, and

- Unable to empower employees and nurture an environment in which they could grow.

I encourage you to watch the show. You'll find a few episodes on YouTube.

Ego is the enemy of success, and pride is the biggest obstacle standing in the way of your personal growth. Whenever you become defensive or refuse to admit you might be wrong, you rob yourself of an opportunity to make changes that could improve your results.

Sure, you can certainly achieve success with a huge ego, but it will likely be to the detriment of people around you. Note that ego is fear-based. People with big egos often rule by fear. On the other hand, people who can let go of their ego tend to encourage others, inspiring them to become better.

Being able to let go of your ego and accept the idea that you don't know everything will allow you to learn faster and make better decisions. Remember, wanting to be right or being in denial will prevent you from absorbing the information you need to refine your current model of reality.

Therefore, let go of your ego (at least a little bit), listen to the people around you and admit when you're wrong or don't have all the answers. Then, use your enhanced model of reality to make wiser decisions.

* * *

Action step

How is pride preventing you from living the life you want? Write your answers in your action guide.

SECTION IX

DEVELOPING EMOTIONAL RESILIENCE

Do not judge me by my success, judge me by how many times I fell down and got back up again.

— NELSON MANDELA, POLITICAL LEADER.

Your ability to become emotionally resilient and to remain optimistic over a long period of time is key to your future success. We often fall prey to negativity, giving up prematurely when the going gets tough. However, we have the power within us to keep going. We can develop perseverance and resilience far beyond anything we can imagine.

As you learn to take better control of your emotions, you'll find yourself persevering when you would have previously given up. And the more you learn to persevere, the easier it will become. Emotional resilience is a skill and, in this section, we're going to see how you can cultivate it.

Let's get started, shall we?

78

EMBRACE PATIENCE

 Patience and fortitude conquer all things.

— RALPH WALDO EMERSON, ESSAYIST AND PHILOSOPHER.

You've been lied to.

You've been told you can lose thirty pounds, make $10,000 per month or develop a six-pack easily and effortlessly. And if you fail, it's because something is wrong with you.

I have good news for you. Nothing is wrong with you.

You have the ability to achieve almost anything you set your mind to. However, let's face the truth: it's going to be way harder than any marketer might be telling you.

Most people overestimate what they can accomplish in a few months but underestimate what they're capable of accomplishing in a few years. Life is a marathon, not a sprint. As such, you must play the long game. You must remain patient in the pursuit of your dreams. Never lose sight of the bigger picture. Forget about short-term gimmicks and tricks. Instead, develop a rock-solid routine that includes powerful habits (see *Chapter 21. Create a morning ritual* and *Chapter 70. Build and maintain consistency*).

A major point to understand is that success is rarely a linear process. It grows exponentially. You might work for months without seeing many results, but at some point, you will start seeing improvement—and these will often be exponential.

Therefore, learn to develop patience. Keep the big picture in mind and constantly remind yourself to be patient. Do this as often as necessary. Forget about attaining overnight success. In almost all cases, people who achieve "instant" success have been grinding away for years, failing over and over, and refining their craft behind the scenes. They stuck to the process, believing their time would come.

To cultivate patience, you must understand how the process called "success" works. This will provide you with the confidence and belief needed to embrace patience. Put differently, once you have a fairly accurate model of reality and know what you need to do every day, you'll have faith in the process and will be able to remain patient if and when things go south.

So, keep reading this book and deepen your understanding of the way success works. Then, set the right process that will allow you to achieve your long-term goals. And, more importantly, *be patient*.

* * *

Action step

Remind yourself to be patient and read this book as often as necessary until you have a solid grasp of the principles introduced in it.

79

TREAT EACH DAY AS A NEW BEGINNING

 The best thing about the future is that it comes one day at a time.

— ABRAHAM LINCOLN, FORMER PRESIDENT OF THE UNITED STATES.

Are you making today count? Or are you taking the oncoming day for granted?

Today is the most important day for you. This is because your life is nothing more than a succession of "todays". Yesterday is gone. Tomorrow has yet to come. Today is all you have.

Sadly, many of us go through life on autopilot. We disrespect the day in front of us by taking it for granted. As a result, we fail to make it count. We're too busy worrying about the past or the future to truly savor the present day and take inspired actions that move us toward our goals. This sometimes makes us feel as though we're reliving the same day over and over again, as in the movie Groundhog Day—but without the happy ending.

But it doesn't have to be this way.

You can make each day count to the max. You can start your day by being excited and full of enthusiasm. You can see today as an opportunity to make different decisions and take new actions that will change your life for the better.

I invite you to stop being casual with your day. Because *when you're casual with your day, you're casual with your life*. Instead, treat the oncoming day with the greatest respect. See each new day as an independent unit—a 24-hour long life, if you will. Then, make it count.

Here are a few tips to make each day count:

- **Smile.** As soon as you wake up, smile. This simple act will boost your mood over time.
- **Act.** Don't hit the snooze button. Jump out of bed immediately. This will help build the habit of being proactive and decisive.
- **Acknowledge.** Think how lucky you are to have been granted a new day. This is the first step to making your day count.
- **Clear.** Start your day as a blank canvas. To do so, visualize yourself letting go of the burden of your past. For instance, picture your past as a ball and chain. Break free from your chains and feel yourself becoming lighter and lighter. This will help you be more present during the day.
- **Express gratitude.** Think of three things you're grateful for or do one of the exercises introduced in *Chapter 85. Cultivate gratitude*. This will boost your mood and reduce your negative emotions.
- **Plan.** Write down today's date as well as your goals for the day. This will help you give more importance to your day while boosting your productivity.

By going through this simple process every day, you'll feel more present and get more out of your day. So, treat each day as a new beginning. Make today count. It's all you have.

See also *Chapter 37. Cultivate optimism*, *Chapter 58. Set daily goals* and *Chapter 64. Focus on the process*.

* * *

Action step

For the next few days, experiment with the process above (smile, act, acknowledge, clear, express gratitude, and plan). See how it makes you feel.

80

FOCUS ON WHAT YOU CAN CONTROL

 Do what you can, with what you have, where you are.

— THEODORE ROOSEVELT, FORMER PRESIDENT OF THE
UNITED STATES.

How much time do you spend worrying about things over which you have no control? If you're like most people, probably way too much time.

Your time and energy are extremely scarce. Every second you spend worrying could have been better spent taking constructive action to solve your challenges. This is time you will never get back.

The truth is, life can be rather unpredictable. You may get sick, lose your job or break up with your spouse or partner. The economy may crash tomorrow, or a natural disaster may damage your house. Many things are out of your control. Focusing on these things will do nothing to improve your life. It will only create unnecessary mental suffering.

Now, before you even start worrying, it is important to realize that in life, "problems" fall into one of the following three categories:

1. Things you have total control over,
2. Things you have some control over, and
3. Things you have no control over whatsoever.

Logically speaking, you may understand there is no point wasting your time and energy worrying about things you have zero control over (#3). Yet, you may still be spending a lot of time doing so. To avoid excessive worry, remember these three categories. Over time, you want to cultivate the habit of categorizing your issues and acting accordingly.

To do so, ask yourself the following questions:

- Do I have control over the situation?
- If so, what could I do about it? (brainstorming phase)
- What exactly will I do about it? (writing down specific action steps)

The more you train yourself to categorize issues (control/some control/no control) and act accordingly, the less time you will waste worrying and the more effective your actions will become. So, stop worrying about things you have no control over. Don't replay the scene over and over in your mind. When you do so, you tell your mind to remember your worries—and the associated emotions— permanently. You don't want to give that power to your worries, do you? Instead, focus on things you have control over. Whenever you face a problem, ask yourself, "What can I do about it?" Then, take action to solve it. For all the rest, let go (see also *Chapter 36. Focus on what you want* and *Chapter 64. Focus on the process*).

* * *

Action step

Using the table in your action guide, take a couple of minutes to write a few things you're worrying about. Then, in the right-hand column, write down whether you have total control (TC) some control (SC) or no control (NC) over the situation.

81

LEVERAGE THE POWER OF REFRAMING

 If you change the way you look at things, the things you look at change.

— WAYNE DYER, PSYCHOLOGIST AND AUTHOR.

It's not what's happening to you that determines the quality of your life, it's the meaning you give to it.

Your mind can't help but assign meaning to any situation. The good news is that you have the power to reframe any situation. For instance, when you face hardships, you can see yourself as a victim, believing the world is against you, or you can choose to believe these hardships are here to teach you invaluable lessons that will allow you to grow. It's all a matter of perspective.

Successful people tend to be intentional in the way they interpret events. Instead of seeing themselves as victims, they aim to give empowering meanings to an event. Below are some useful questions you can ask yourself to reframe any situation:

- What's great about it?
- What valuable lesson can I learn from it?

- What shortcomings does it invite me to overcome?
- In what way(s) does this situation invite me to become my best self?
- What qualities does it demand I develop further?
- How can I turn this situation into an opportunity rather than seeing it as an obstacle?

The key lesson here is, learn to reframe life's challenges as character-building events rather than dream-crushing ones. Do this and you'll be well on your way to achieving your biggest goals (see also *Chapter 37. Cultivate optimism* and *Chapter 52. Cultivate long-term thinking*).

Your ability to remain optimistic is massively important. Reframing situations will help you maintain a positive state of mind and take more actions toward your goals. Remember, your ability to reframe will improve with practice, and as you keep practicing, over time it will become easier and easier.

* * *

Action step

Think of one negative event that happened to you recently. Then, ask yourself:

- What was great about it?
- What valuable lesson did/could I learn from it?
- How did I turn (or how could I have turned) this situation into an opportunity?

82

HONOR THE STRUGGLE

> Suffering is but another name for the teaching of experience, which is the parent of instruction and the schoolmaster of life.

— HORACE, ROMAN POET.

Do you struggle to achieve your goals? Are you disappointed by your results? Have your expectations been crushed repeatedly?

Struggles are inevitable, but the way you deal with them is entirely up to you. The path toward success is made of mountains and valleys, and the process is often chaotic. You can deny this fact and complain every time problems occur, or...

...you can honor the struggle.

Honoring the struggle means that you learn to appreciate the process that leads to success. Once they "made it", people often remember earlier times with a sense of nostalgia. They wished they had let themselves enjoy the process more.

Now, I understand it is easier to feel that way *after* the fact, not while you're struggling and wondering whether you'll ever make it. Yet, there are lessons to be learned here.

First, acknowledge your effort and value the process itself, not the results it will lead to. The process will help you grow and become a better person. The fact you're sticking to it is already a sign of success.

Second, realize that struggles—and your ability to embrace them and overcome them—will separate you from other people who will throw in the towel. Every time you persevere, you differentiate yourself from quitters who are not serious about their goals.

Third, often the real value of a goal is not in its achievement, but it's in the person you have to become to reach it.

The bottom line is, struggle isn't an anomaly. It isn't the opposite of success. It's part of the process. So, why not acknowledge yourself for having the courage to move toward your dreams?

You will struggle. The question is, what are you going to do about it?

See also *Chapter 41. Celebrate your success* and *Chapter 83. Cultivate self-compassion.*

* * *

Action step

Remember the difficult times you had to go through to reach your current position. In hindsight, what would you say to your past self? Then, say the same thing to your present self and see how it feels.

83

CULTIVATE SELF-COMPASSION

 Talk to yourself like someone you love.

— Brené Brown, research professor and author.

Are you your own worst critic? Do you keep beating yourself up for each small mistake you make?

Now, imagine if you talked to your family or friends the way you talk to yourself. How would they react? Would they feel loved and respected?

Many people buy into the idea that being harsh on ourselves is the right way to go, but this comes from a lack of self-trust. Deep down, we don't believe we'll get work done unless we use the carrot and stick approach. However, is this true? Have you ever tried to talk to yourself in a more gentle and respectful way? If so, what happened? Did you suddenly become lazy?

In truth, beating yourself up is counterproductive. It doesn't help you be more productive, but it does make you feel bad about yourself. Now, imagine if you could talk to yourself like a skillful coach does. Imagine if you were to become your best supporter. Wouldn't you feel more motivated? I believe you would. In fact, I want to challenge you to talk to yourself in a compassionate way for the next seven days. Whenever you feel the urge to criticize yourself, be self-compassionate instead. Let's say you've forgotten an appointment. Rather than telling yourself how stupid you are, you could say to yourself something like:

"It's okay. We all make mistakes and forget appointments occasionally. In the future, I'll be more careful. I'm going to apologize and then I'll take some action to avoid the same thing happening next time."

The point is, as an imperfect human being, you are bound to make mistakes and to fall short of your goals, and you'll do it many times. But this is not a reason to beat yourself up and make yourself miserable. And it's certainly not a reason to give up on your goals, or worse, on yourself.

Do not use self-criticism as a motivational tool. Instead, use self-compassion. Forgive yourself for your missteps. Keep encouraging yourself. Life can be hard. Don't make it harder by being overly tough on yourself.

You're doing okay.

* * *

Action step

For the next seven days, speak to yourself only in a gentle, supportive way. Whenever you're harsh with yourself notice it and refocus on being kind to yourself.

84

PREPARE FOR THE WORST

 Before anything else, preparation is the key to success.

— ALEXANDER GRAHAM BELL, INVENTOR.

Life is unpredictable. The best way to deal with what life throws at us is to be prepared to face almost anything. It's easy to give up when the going gets tough. Often, the reason we throw in the towel is because we had unrealistic expectations to begin with. We believed going from where we are to where we want to be would be a breeze—but it seldom, if ever, is.

This is when preparing for the worse can be useful. Imagine if you had already envisioned all the worst-case scenarios you can think of and were mentally prepared to deal with them. Wouldn't that be helpful?

This is what preparing for the worst is about.

For instance, will you be okay if you don't make any money for two years with your new business? What will you do if you publish seven books but none of them takes off? What about barely losing weight after a month of dieting?

The reason this method is effective is because it allows you to project yourself into the future and decide how to react if things don't turn out exactly as planned. It's a little bit like rehearsing before a show.

Now, you don't need to worry excessively about these worst-case scenarios. Once you've been through them in your mind a few times, return your focus to what you want in your life (see *Chapter 36. Focus on what you want*). From time to time, remind yourself of potential worst-case scenarios. By doing so, you won't be taken by surprise when something unexpected happens, and you will be able to bounce back quickly.

Yes, sometimes bad things do happen, but you have the ability to maintain a positive state of mind and stick to your process even when everything around you seems to be falling apart. This level of determination will allow you to achieve most of your goals long term.

* * *

Action step

Think of one major goal you're currently working toward and write down some of the worst-case scenarios you can think of. Then, imagine yourself going through each of them. What would be your initial reaction? Finally, see yourself pushing through these obstacles.

85

PRACTICE GRATITUDE

 The struggle ends when gratitude begins.

— NEALE DONALD WALSCH, AUTHOR AND SPEAKER.

Do you take the time to appreciate all the wonderful things you have going for you?

I believe gratitude is one of the most powerful forces on earth. While there may not seem to be a direct correlation with gratitude and success, in reality, your ability to be grateful will often dramatically improve your results. This is because being able to remain in a positive state of mind is a key component of long-term success. When you feel good about yourself, you are more creative, more productive, and much happier. You become less prone to negative self-talk and can move more freely toward your goals.

Now, you might have been told many times that you should be grateful for what you have. Or you may understand intellectually that you're fortunate in so many ways. Perhaps your health is excellent. Perhaps you have a number of really close friends. Perhaps you have a wonderful relationship with your partner or a career you enjoy. But knowing something intellectually isn't the same thing as *feeling* it. Theoretical knowledge is useless without practice.

Gratitude needs to be practiced. To cultivate deeper feelings of gratitude, I encourage you to adopt daily gratitude exercises. An effective way to do so is to include them in your morning ritual (see also *Chapter 21. Create a morning ritual*).

Below are some daily exercises you can experiment with:

- **Write down what you're grateful for.** Write down three things you're grateful for and try to come up with three different things every day.
- **Create a gratitude journal.** Buy a notebook and use it to record any compliments you receive. Keep adding new entries and go through old ones every day, or at least a few times a week.
- **Thank people.** Close your eyes and think of the first person that comes to mind. Then, thank that person (in your mind). Try to thank them for at least one specific thing they did for you. Perhaps they helped you find a job. Perhaps they were there for you during challenging times. Perhaps they taught you a lesson. Repeat the process with a second person. Keep doing this for three to five minutes. To help you experience feelings of gratitude, you can listen to a song that moves you while doing this exercise.

As you keep practicing gratitude every day, you'll start feeling better and better. And, as your emotional state improves, you'll find yourself taking new actions that will improve your life.

So, what are all the things you're grateful for?

* * *

Action step

- Think of ten things you're the most grateful for right now.
- Adopt a daily gratitude practice using one of the exercises introduced above.

86
___

LEARN FROM YOUR EMOTIONS

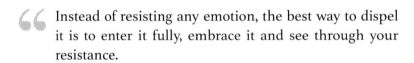 Instead of resisting any emotion, the best way to dispel it is to enter it fully, embrace it and see through your resistance.

— DEEPAK CHOPRA, AUTHOR.

Do you know what would happen if you were unable to feel physical pain?

The risk to your life would increase exponentially.

Pain is the way your body signals you that something is wrong and that you need to do something about it. Emotions act in a similar way. They aren't here to make your life harder but to guide you. Thus, instead of seeing negative emotions as bad, why not try to learn from them?

Maybe you feel unhappy. If so, why do you think this is the case? Is it because you hate your job? Is it because you don't have much of a social life? Is it because you're hanging out with the wrong people?

Or maybe you resent someone. If so, why is that? Is it a sign you should have a heart-to-heart conversation with that person? Is it an invitation to adopt a new way of thinking and let go of resentment?

Any feeling you experience is a wonderful opportunity to learn more about yourself. Negative emotions can be a sign you're living a life out of alignment with your values, personality or purpose. They can indicate that you must go beyond your comfort zone and face someone or something you're afraid of. Or they can tell you that you need to develop more self-compassion.

All that is to say, there is nothing wrong with negative emotions. They're simply here to tell you that you might be going off track, inviting you to make different choices to increase your happiness.

Below are some examples of lessons you could learn from specific emotions.

Resentment:

- Understanding that your peace of mind is more important than taking revenge,
- Developing the courage to share your feelings with other people (instead of building up resentment), and
- Learning not to take anything personally (what people do to you often has nothing to do with you).

Defensiveness:

- Seeking the truth in something someone said to you (you may feel hurt because they're shedding the light on something you would rather ignore),
- Identifying the underlying beliefs that lead you to act defensively, and
- Learning to let go of these beliefs.

Dissatisfaction:

- Clarifying your values and attempting to live by them,

- Becoming assertive and not tolerating the way certain people treat you anymore, and
- Stopping seeking people's approval and doing what feels right to you.

As you can see, there are tons of things to learn from your negative emotions. So instead of seeing them as bad, seize every opportunity to learn more about yourself so that you can become a better person.

To learn more about how to use your emotions as a tool for your personal growth, you can refer to my book, *Master Your Emotions: A Practical Guide to Overcome Negativity and Better Manage Your Feelings.*

* * *

Action step

Think of one negative emotion you experienced recently. Now ask yourself, "What can I learn from that particular emotion? What is it trying to tell me?"

87

——————

EXERCISE REGULARLY

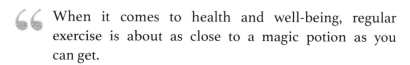 When it comes to health and well-being, regular exercise is about as close to a magic potion as you can get.

— THICH NHAT HANH, BUDDHIST MONK AND PEACE ACTIVIST.

Do you exercise regularly?

Exercise is a powerful mood enhancer and can definitely help you manage your feelings better. Exercise can also make you more resilient.

Studies have shown that exercising can be as powerful as an antidepressant. Dr. Michael Craig Miller, assistant professor of psychiatry at Harvard Medical School, said the following about exercise, *"For some people it works as well as antidepressants, although exercise alone isn't enough for someone with severe depression."*

In his book, *Constructive Living*, David Reynold explains how he purposefully created depression in order to be put in a mental institution. His goal was to observe the effectiveness of the care given to patients.

Do you know what he had to do to get out of his (clinically proven) depression? He had to force himself to engage in physical activity. The point is, physical activity is a powerful way to maintain emotional well-being.

In addition to exercise being a powerful antidepressant, it has tons of other health benefits. Even just regular brisk walking is beneficial to our health. According to the Mayo Clinic, brisk walking can help you maintain a healthy weight, help fight heart disease, reduce high-blood pressure and it can help fight many other serious conditions. Regular exercise can also improve your mood. And even better, you don't have to exercise heavily. Just engaging in regular brisk walking for forty-five minutes, three to four times per week, can have tremendous health benefits.

In the book, *Spark: How Exercise Will Improve the Performance of Your Brain*, Dr. John J. Ratey and Eric Hagerman wrote the following, *"Exercise has a profound impact on cognitive abilities and mental health. It is simply one of the best treatments we have for most psychiatric problems."*

Exercise is not only beneficial to your health, but it also boosts your mood and enhances your cognitive abilities. So, unless medical reasons prevent you from exercising, I highly recommend you put in place an exercise routine.

Note that if you can't exercise properly, there are still many things you might be able to do to enhance your mood and stay healthy whether it is meditating, stretching, or practicing breathing techniques to name a few.

* * *

Action step

Using your action guide, write down a simple exercise routine you could see yourself following for months or years. Remember that being consistent is key. Start small. You can always intensify your workout over time.

SECTION X

INFLUENCING AND INSPIRING OTHERS

There is nothing noble in being superior to your fellow man; true nobility is being superior to your former self.

— ERNEST HEMINGWAY, NOVELIST.

Nobody is self-made. We all build our individual success with the help of others. Therefore, our ability to influence or inspire others is critical. In this final section, we'll see what you can do to inspire others. We'll discover why it is important to help others in order to get what you want.

88

SHARE YOUR DREAMS/BROADCAST YOUR DESIRES

 Successful and unsuccessful people do not vary greatly in their abilities. They vary in their desires to reach their potential.

— JOHN MAXWELL, AUTHOR, SPEAKER AND LEADERSHIP EXPERT.

Does the universe know what you want?

Because if it doesn't, it won't be able to help you.

There are over seven billion people on this planet and millions of them have the resources you need to achieve your wildest goals and dreams—whether it is money, time, skills, or networks. Why not take advantage of these things?

Many people believe they can't achieve their goals because they lack the resources. However, as the success coach, Tony Robbins, said, you don't lack resources, what you lack is resourcefulness. If you believe you can't find the resources you need, you're selling yourself short, forgetting your mind is the most powerful machine ever created.

As the blogger, Steve Pavlina, puts it, often, the first step toward gathering the resources you need to achieve your biggest goals is simply to broadcast your desires.

After all, how are people supposed to help you if they don't know what you need?

Many people are willing to support you on your journey toward your dreams. Remember, people like to be followers or supporters (e.g., think of sports fans). They enjoy supporting people who have ambitious dreams. But, to be able to help you, they must know what you aim to achieve.

Below are some of the things that will determine whether people might agree to help you:

- **Your level of clarity.** People want to know exactly what you want and why you want it.
- **Your level of enthusiasm.** People are more willing to help you if they feel you're genuinely excited about your goals (who doesn't want more excitement in his or her life?).
- **Your level of commitment.** People need to see you're committed. For instance, successful people will not waste their time helping you unless they're sure you'll do what it takes to reach your goals.
- **Your actions.** People must see you taking consistent action and obtaining early results. When they project your current actions onto the future, they should believe you have a reasonable chance of achieving your goals, or at least you have a good chance of making significant progress toward your vision.

The bottom line is, when you gain clarity regarding your goals, commit to going after them and broadcast them to the world, and the universe will often help you achieve them.

So, share your dreams with the world and get started now.

* * *

Action step

What goal could you broadcast to the world and how will you do it?

89

SEE YOURSELF AS A ROLE MODEL

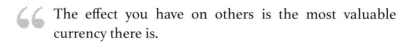 The effect you have on others is the most valuable currency there is.

— JIM CARREY, ACTOR.

How many people have improved their lives as a result of being around you? If the answer is none, why is that?

One of the golden rules of personal development is that anybody who crosses your path should be better off for having met you. At least, this is what I believe you should strive for.

The truth is that nobody changes simply because you ask them to. They change because of who you are. Furthermore, the actions you take speak louder than your words. People change because they feel inspired and want to be like you in some way.

When you see yourself as a role model and strive to become a better version of yourself, you'll find that people around you start to grow, too. This is a sign you're on the right path. So, ask yourself what being a role model means to you. How do you want people around you to improve? And what inner change do you need to make so that they feel inspired to follow your path?

You cannot control what's outside you, but you can control how you behave. So, act the way you would like other people to act. Not because you're deluded enough to believe you can change the world, but because you have enough respect for yourself to do what you believe is right.

You may not impact the world around you in a major way, but at least you'll be able to look yourself in the mirror, knowing you're doing the right thing. And what's more, you'll feel good about yourself for staying true to your values.

So, start seeing yourself as a role model. To paraphrase Gandhi, be the change you wish to see in the world. Because, if you're not embodying the changes you want to witness in the future, who will follow you?

See also *Chapter 23. Respect yourself* and *Chapter 34. Believe that who you are and what you do matters.*

* * *

Action step

Answer the following questions:

- Who has changed for the better as a result of spending time around me?
- What could I do specifically to become an even better source of inspiration to the people around me?

90

AIM TO CHANGE YOURSELF BEFORE CHANGING OTHERS

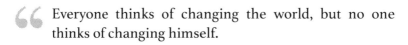 Everyone thinks of changing the world, but no one thinks of changing himself.

— LEO TOLSTOY, WRITER.

Do you have a burning desire to make a huge impact on the world?

If so, I have bad news for you: you will have to work harder on yourself than on anything else. Often, people try to change the world, but have little understanding of themselves. They're unsure of their strengths and weaknesses and ignore their personal blind spots and biases. They don't realize to what extent their thinking is flawed and have little to no awareness of their limiting beliefs.

Trying to change the world before understanding yourself is seldom a good idea and can create more problems than it solves. Without enough self-awareness, your model of reality will be highly inaccurate. As a result, your decisions will mostly be wrong and your actions will either be ineffective or actively counterproductive. In fact, being unable to align yourself with reality can be dangerous. Examples of people misaligned with reality are religious extremists and other ideologists. Smart people living only in the world of ideas can wreak havoc on society when put in positions of power.

Developing self-awareness is the first step to changing yourself—and perhaps the world. The second step is continuously working on your personal growth. Because, in the end, the impact you can have on the world is largely limited by how much control you have over your mind. Think about it. How will you bring about major changes in the world if you have no self-discipline, little confidence, poor leadership skills, weak social skills and no control over your emotions?

Therefore, if you're serious about making an impact on the world, work on yourself like never before. Continually and diligently work toward cultivating self-awareness. Develop a profound understanding of your own psychology. Strive for a better understanding of how your mind works. By doing so, you'll be able to take better and wiser actions, actions that will have a more profound impact on society.

The bottom line is this: if you want to become an influential person who makes things happen in this world, work on your personal growth. Boost your confidence, build your self-discipline, increase your self-awareness, improve your communication skills, improve your health, and so on. In short, never stop working on yourself. Then, perhaps you'll end up changing the world—at least a little.

* * *

Action step

Answer the following question:

If I were to change something within myself, what specific thing would allow me to have the biggest possible impact on the world around me?

91

ADD VALUE TO OTHER PEOPLE'S LIVES

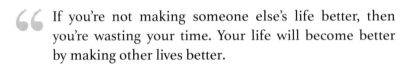 If you're not making someone else's life better, then you're wasting your time. Your life will become better by making other lives better.

— WILL SMITH, ACTOR.

How much time do you spend thinking of ways you can serve others?

Many people look for ways to make money without having to work for it. They're always looking for the next get-rich-quick scheme. These people don't seem to understand how money works. Saying you want to make money without working for it means you want others to part with their hard-earned money and give it to you—without delivering them any value.

This is unlikely to happen.

The only way to generate money that way is to scam people. You might make money, at least in the short term, but is it how you want to live your life? Wouldn't you rather add real value to people's lives?

When it comes to success, one of the most important questions you can ever ask yourself is simply, "How can I help?" This is a magical question. Ask yourself this question daily for long enough, and you will end up serving far more people, while making more money in the process (assuming this is what you want).

Bear in mind this is anything but a scheme. Constantly serving others is a long-term strategy that will enhance your happiness—because helping others makes you feel good—and skyrockets your success.

Another benefit of asking yourself this question is that it will require you grow and develop new skills. After all, how can you provide more value without becoming better yourself?

So, start becoming more valuable and keep thinking of ways to deliver more and more value to the people around you. Do this for long enough and you'll be able to have most of the things you want. What will you do to deliver more value to people around you?

* * *

Action step

Answer the following question:

How can I deliver more value to the people around me?

92

BELIEVE IN THE POTENTIAL OF OTHERS

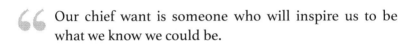 Our chief want is someone who will inspire us to be what we know we could be.

— RALPH WALDO EMERSON, ESSAYIST AND PHILOSOPHER.

Do you see others for who they could be or for who they are right now with all their fears and limitations?

Most people are playing it small. They've erected artificial walls around themselves, and they are blind to their incredible potential and amazing abilities. They confine themselves inside a small box, and they will often stay inside that box for the rest of their lives.

The point I'm making here is that people around you have more potential than you can imagine. So, instead of focusing on their limitations, why not see them for who they could become? Life is a mystery. People will sometimes "wake up" and start uncovering their own potential. All they need is a nudge. They need someone who can see in them what they cannot see yet—someone who believes in their potential.

Be that person.

Refuse to buy into people's excuses. See beyond the story they're telling themselves. Look for their unique talents and strengths that, when developed, could change everything both for them and for the people around them. Keep seeing them for who they could become and, maybe, they will bloom. Now, there is no guarantee it will ever happen, but I invite you to give the gift of belief to the people around you. Plant the seed of potential in them. Then, let them decide what to do with it.

Expect everybody around you to become happier and more successful. Keep believing in them. By believing in people you will enhance the impact you can have on the world. And the upside is, you will feel good whenever you see someone overcoming their limitations and becoming better versions of themselves.

Believe in the potential of others more than they believe in themselves, then watch them grow over time.

* * *

Action step

Close your eyes and visualize the people close to you (family members, friends, colleagues, et cetera). For each person you visualize, imagine them as having achieved their absolute potential. Envision how they would feel, think and act. See all the wonderful things they would be accomplishing.

93

BE OBSESSED WITH YOUR CUSTOMERS

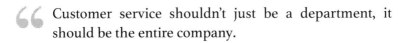 Customer service shouldn't just be a department, it should be the entire company.

— TONY HSIEH, ENTREPRENEUR.

How often do you think of your customers? How much do you truly care about them?

The only *raison d'être* for a business is to serve its customers. It sounds obvious but it's worth repeating. A business isn't about you; it's about your customers or clients.

This means you must try to understand your customers better and give them what they want, not what you *think* they want. As a business owner or employee, your job isn't to come up with fancy ideas. What matters, ultimately, is whether your customers are willing to part with their money to buy your products or services. Without your customers, you have no business. Note that I'm not saying you can't work on things you love, but that you should do so in a way that serves your customers.

You should also strive to over-deliver on your promises. For instance,

Amazon is known for delivering packages faster than they promised. The way they do this is by setting a delivery schedule they can beat every time. Whatever services you or your company is offering, make sure to under-promise and over-deliver—not the other way around.

Now, if you're an employee, your supervisor is also your customer. The better you understand what he/she wants and over-deliver on it, the more likely you are to be seen as a valuable employee—and eventually earn your promotion. For instance, try to answer the following questions:

- What are my supervisor's goals?
- What will my supervisor be evaluated on?
- What would my supervisor do if he/she were in my shoes?
- How can I make my supervisor's work easier?

If you don't know the answers, try to ask your supervisor how you can make his/her work easier.

The more you understand what your customers/supervisors require, the better you can meet their needs—and the better results you'll obtain.

Be obsessed with your customers.

* * *

Action step

Answer the following question:

How can you give your customers what they truly want?

94

COMPLIMENT OTHERS

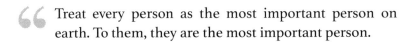 Treat every person as the most important person on earth. To them, they are the most important person.

— Earl Nightingale, radio host and author.

When was the last time you complimented someone?

People crave compliments. This is why I invite you to practice giving genuine compliments to the people around you. Sometimes, one small compliment can make someone's day. A few words of encouragement at the right time can even change their lives.

There are several reasons that giving compliments can be beneficial both for the receiver and for the giver. Let's look at each of them.

1. Giving compliments make other people feel appreciated

Most of us want to feel appreciated. We love receiving compliments. Compliments can enhance our self-esteem and boost our mood. For instance, a simple "good job" can motivate us to work even harder on the next task. In fact, it is often the small words repeated every day that make a difference, not the big compliments given once in a while. So, aim to compliment others whenever the opportunity presents itself. It only takes you a few seconds, but can impact others in a major way.

2. Giving compliments allows us to appreciate others better

By continually looking for ways to compliment others, we find more and more reasons to appreciate these people, which can improve the quality of our relationships. For example, genuine compliments exchanged with your partner on a regular basis can lead you to better appreciate him/her, and vice-versa.

3. Giving compliments trains us to look for the good

Because of the way our mind is wired, we tend to focus on the negative. As we practice finding the good in others, we become better at finding the good in ourselves. Also, by mustering the courage to compliment others, we give ourselves permission to love ourselves more and acknowledge our wins and positive intentions as well.

The bottom line is, treat every person as the most important person on earth because, to them, they are. Compliment them genuinely, try to appreciate their efforts and give them a little of your attention rather than taking them for granted.

Giving compliments cost you nothing but can mean everything to the receiver. So, why not practice giving compliments, starting today?

* * *

Action step

Think of five people you spend a lot of time with and give one genuine compliment to each of them (in your mind). Try to think of something you've never told them before. Then, challenge yourself to give them that compliment in real life.

95

SEEK A WIN-WIN

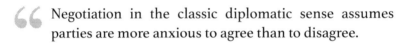 Negotiation in the classic diplomatic sense assumes parties are more anxious to agree than to disagree.

— DEAN ACHESON, FORMER STATESMAN.

Your ability to put yourself in the shoes of the other person is extremely important during any kind of negotiation. You can certainly try to win and give as little as possible to your counterpart, but is that sustainable? Furthermore, is it even a good idea?

For any relationship to last long term, it is necessary for both sides to believe they're getting their fair share. Therefore, instead of trying to get the best deal and only thinking of your own interests, endeavor to create win-win situations every time you work with others.

Ask yourself:

- How can I make this situation a win-win?
- How can I give the other side what they want while still getting what I want?

For this to be possible you must actually understand what the other side wants. Not just what they say they want, but what they actually value the most and care about. No effective negotiation is possible unless you're able to identify what people you negotiate with want.

You also need to be open to the possibility that both parties can get what they want. Then, you must be determined to create a win-win situation. To do so, rather than seeing the pie as fixed, think of ways to create a bigger pie. Can you offer something extra that your counterpart will value but that doesn't cost you much? Can you make some concessions by asking for something else you value, but that they don't?

Trying to create win-win situations can become a habit. As you keep practicing, you'll become better at it.

* * *

Action step

Think of someone with whom you are having a disagreement. What could you do to create a win-win relationship with that person?

96

ASK MORE QUESTIONS, GIVE FEWER ANSWERS

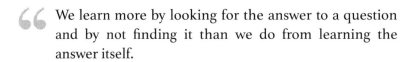 We learn more by looking for the answer to a question and by not finding it than we do from learning the answer itself.

— LLOYD ALEXANDER, AUTHOR.

Do you know how to ask smart questions?

The main reason people hire coaches or consultants is because they want to be asked the right questions (*see also Chapter 55. Ask smart questions*). Questions invite us to think deeply and, as a result, come up with ingenious solutions. As such, they are invaluable.

By asking people questions, you help them think and organize their ideas in a coherent fashion, which enhances their creativity and boosts their motivation (among other things). You also help them come up with solutions to their own problems.

Sadly, instead of helping people organize their thoughts by asking them questions, many people give them advice. For instance, they tell them what they believe they should do or how they should think. Unfortunately, feeding people fish isn't the same as teaching them how to fish. Giving them answers doesn't help them become effective thinkers, neither does it help them solve their problems.

Another reason asking questions is powerful is because it creates buy-in. For instance, a person is far more likely to take action if they come up with the idea themselves. After all, nobody likes to be told what to do. People want to feel as though they devised the idea or solution themselves.

The point is, just because (you think) you know the right answer, doesn't mean you should give it to someone. It is often more effective to ask questions and let people come up with their own answers. This way, they will be more motivated to take action.

Now, there are situations where you should probably give people answers. For instance, if you know from experience that something doesn't work, don't let someone go down that path and waste months of their lives. But, whenever relevant, learn to ask people smart questions. More importantly, let them think for themselves. Don't fear pauses. Welcome them. If people need time to think, it's usually a sign that the question you're asking is powerful. Rather than interrupting them, give them time to come up with their own solutions. They will feel empowered, listened to, and valued.

Ask more questions and give less advice. Then, see how it changes your relationships with the people around you.

* * *

Action step

Today, notice whenever you feel like giving an answer or offering advice. Then, pause and ask yourself what question you could ask instead.

97

LISTEN MORE, TALK LESS

> " When you talk, you are only repeating what you
> already know. But if you listen, you may learn
> something new.

— DALAI LAMA, SPIRITUAL LEADER.

When was the last time you actually listened to someone?

Most people think they listen. They most likely don't. Listening is an active process that requires concentration. It is *not* easy. As Steven Covey wrote in, *The 7 Habits of Highly Effective People*, most people don't listen to understand, they listen only to reply.

The ability to listen is far more important than most people think. The reason people work with therapists or coaches is because these people will actually *listen* to them.

I believe there are several reasons you ought to listen more and talk less.

The first reason is because when you practice active listening, people will open up to you more. By listening actively, you show people you respect them and want to understand how they think and feel. Sensing that, people will feel more comfortable expressing their true feelings around you. For example, one of my friends is so skillful at listening that people often share with him things they have never shared before.

The second reason is because you can learn more by listening than by talking. It is said we were given two ears and only one mouth because we should spend twice as much time listening as talking.

The third reason is because practicing active listening will allow you to increase your awareness and enhance your ability to be present in the moment. This is a great mindfulness exercise to practice on a daily basis.

Now, let me share with you what active listening is not. It's *not*:

- **Listening to take control of the conversation**. How often do you try to move the conversation toward a topic you enjoy?
- **Listening to give advice.** Often, people want to be understood. They're not asking for advice so avoid giving them any (unless they ask for it).
- **Thinking of what to say next.** Listening requires you to be fully present. You can't do that when you're already formulating in your mind what to say next.
- **Judging.** Listening isn't trying to interpret what people say. That's only projecting your model of reality onto theirs. Instead, try to understand what they really mean. Be curious.
- **Hearing only words.** Words aren't necessarily what matters the most. Non-verbal communication such as body language, gestures or vocal tonality is often more important. Active listening means being aware of all these things.

So, you thought listening was easy?

Maybe I've changed your mind.

You might now realize that active listening is powerful and can dramatically enhance your communication skills and the depth of your relationships with others.

Why not practice active listening and see how it changes the way you interact with others?

* * *

Action step

Practice active listening during one of your conversations today.

PUT YOURSELF IN THE SHOES OF OTHER PEOPLE

 You can make more friends in two months by becoming interested in other people than you can in two years by trying to get other people interested in you.

— DALE CARNEGIE, WRITER AND LECTURER.

How often do you focus on what others want instead of what you want?

As human beings, we tend to be self-centered. Even when we think of what others want, we often project our own values and desires onto them instead of trying to understand what *they* want.

Developing the ability to put yourself in the shoes of other people is one of the most valuable skills you can develop. Whenever you meet someone, ask yourself, "What are they trying to do? Where are they trying to go? And why is it so important for them?" Then, actually ask them!

Having a deeper understanding of the direction in which people are heading comes with several benefits. First, it will help you understand why they act the way they do, which, in turn, will help you to predict what they may do next. Second, it will enable you to help them get what they want in a much more effective way. As the late Zig Ziglar said, *"You can have everything in life you want, if you will just help other people get what they want."* And you can only do that by knowing what it is they do want.

Think about it. Do you actually know what your spouse wants? What about your best friend? Your colleagues? Have you ever asked them? The truth is, most people have no idea what people close to them really want or crave.

Once you have a better idea of what people want, aim to understand why they want it. In most cases, people's desires coincide with the emotional benefits they'll receive as a result. And this is usually linked to their deeper values.

For instance, someone's goal might be to make more money, but this can be for a variety of reasons. Perhaps this person wants more freedom, or perhaps they seek more security. Alternatively, they might aspire to a higher social status and greater recognition.

You'll only know the answer to this if you understand people's values. In addition, you may discover that there are sometimes better methods they could adopt to live by their most important values. Using this information, you might be able to help them set different and more relevant goals.

Finally, by understanding people's values, you'll be able to relate to them at a deeper level. The more commonalities you have with people, the easier it will be to build rapport and develop long-term relationships.

* * *

Action step

Select three people close to you and try to define their values and goals. Then, go ask them directly. For instance, share your values first and ask them what their values are. Ask them where they see themselves in ten years.

99

SURROUND YOURSELF WITH SUCCESSFUL PEOPLE

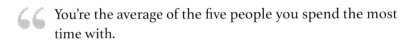 You're the average of the five people you spend the most time with.

— JIM ROHN, BUSINESS PHILOSOPHER.

Let me ask you a question: if you keep your current circle of friends and acquaintances, will you become the person you want to be? In short, are the people around you pushing you to be your best self, or are they holding you back?

Imagine you want to lose weight. Which of the situations below do you think will be the most helpful?

1. Living together with five people who are obsessed with their health and are constantly looking for ways to optimize it.
2. Living together with five people who are overweight and neglect their health.

Your environment plays a key role in your future successes. This is because, as humans, we are like sponges. We absorb the mindset, habits and behaviors of the people around us. This is wonderful when we're surrounded with positive people who encourage us, but it's not so great when we're around negative people who keep telling us our dreams are impossible.

In short, your environment will act either as an anchor that drags you down or as an engine that propels you far beyond anything you can imagine. This all comes down to the type of environment you choose to (or fail to) design.

Therefore, if you want to achieve big dreams, you must upgrade your environment. You must do *whatever it takes* to get away from a negative environment and design a more empowering one.

Dedicate time and effort to creating the most empowering environment possible because, in the long term, relying on willpower alone is unsustainable. This is especially true when you're around people who continuously drag you down. Instead, try to be around growth-oriented people. This will positively impact the way you think, feel, and act, and it will help you grow faster. Choose immersion over willpower.

Remember, there is no reason you can't improve. So, surround yourself with people who expect nothing but the best from you, and keep moving toward your goals.

Action step

Answer the following questions:

- Who is one negative person I want to spend less time with?
- Who is one friend or acquaintance that, if I were to spend more time with, would allow me to grow and learn faster?
- If I could connect with one person to have the most positive impact in the long term, who would it be?

100

FOCUS ON BUILDING LONG-TERM RELATIONSHIPS

 Wishing to be friends is quick work, but friendship is a slow ripening fruit.

— Aristotle, Greek philosopher.

When developing friendships, people tend to focus on the short term. They often hold a specific idea of how they want the other person to help them. For instance, they may connect with them right before a new project, hoping to receive their help. Or, to put it differently, they tend to prioritize the short-term gains rather than seeing how the relationship could evolve long term.

However, it is far more effective to think of people you want to connect with as future friends you plan to hang out with for years. With such a mindset, you're coming from a place of helpfulness. Instead of trying to get something from them, simply connect with them and help them any way you can. Then, allow the relationship to evolve naturally from there.

After all, when you try to make new friends, you don't start by asking them for help or try to sell them something right away, do you? No. You begin by learning more about them. You look for common interests and see how you can create a win-win relationship, (i.e., a relationship you both want to be part of).

Consequently, instead of thinking in terms of networking, strive to build long-term, genuine relationships with people with whom you share common values. Help people you want to work with as much as you can and let the relationships evolve on its own.

* * *

Action step

Answer the following questions using your action guide:

- Who do I want to connect with?
- Specifically, what could I do to help that person?

CONCLUSION

I have to admit that I don't know who you are, where you came from or what specific problems you have. However, I can tell you that, deep inside, you have the potential to grow, to change and to achieve many of your goals and dreams. Over time, I've discovered that success, wealth, happiness and love are mostly a matter of following certain rules. Many people aspire to become wealthy, happy, and successful but, surprisingly, few actually take the time to investigate the way they can achieve them.

But you're different.

You picked up this book and read it through to the end. By doing so, you not only expressed your desire to be more, do more and have more, but you did something about it, too. You showed your willingness to get the most out of the one life you were given, and I sincerely want to congratulate you for doing so. You've demonstrated that you are a serious student of life and, as a result, in the coming weeks, months, and years, you'll be presented fantastic opportunities to grow and design the life you've been dreaming of.

To end this book, I would like to remind you that true success isn't about what you achieve but about who you become in the process of pursuing worthy goals. More importantly, success is about how you improve the lives of other people. It's about becoming a better spouse, parent, friend or colleague. This is why I firmly believe it is your responsibility to reach your fullest potential. You're not helping anybody by making yourself smaller than you really are. So, don't be afraid to embrace change and move toward the life you desire.

Remember, when you change, everything will change for you and around you. This is inevitable. Therefore, take action, face your fears, and become the person you want to be.

What do you think?

I hope you benefit from this book. I would be very grateful if you could take a moment to leave an honest review on Amazon.

Thanks again for your support!

Thibaut

MASTER YOUR EMOTIONS (PREVIEW)

 The mind is its own place, and in itself can make a heaven of Hell, a hell of Heaven.

— JOHN MILTON, POET.

We all experience a wide range of emotions throughout our lives. I had to admit, while writing this book, I experienced highs and lows myself. At first, I was filled with excitement and thrilled at the idea of providing people with a guide to help them understand their emotions. I imagined how readers' lives would improve as they learned to control their emotions. My motivation was high and I couldn't help but imagine how great the book would be.

Or so I thought.

After the initial excitement, the time came to sit down to write the actual book, and that's when the excitement wore off pretty quickly. Suddenly ideas that looked great in my mind felt dull. My writing seemed boring, and I felt as though I had nothing substantive or valuable to contribute.

Sitting at my desk and writing became more challenging each day. I started losing confidence. Who was I to write a book about emotions if I couldn't even master my own emotions? How ironic! I considered giving up. There are already plenty of books on the topic, so why add one more?

At the same time, I realized this book was a perfect opportunity to work on my emotional issues. And who doesn't suffer from negative emotions from time to time? We all have highs and lows, don't we? The key is what we *do* with our lows. Are we using our emotions to grow and learn or are we beating ourselves up over them?

So, let's talk about *your* emotions now. Let me start by asking you this:

How do you feel right now?

Knowing how you feel is the first step toward taking control of your emotions. You may have spent so much time internalizing you've lost touch with your feelings. Perhaps you answered as follows: "I feel this book could be useful," or "I really feel I could learn something from this book."

However, none of these answers reflect on how you feel. You don't 'feel like this,' or 'feel like that,' you simply 'feel.' You don't 'feel like' this book could be useful, you 'think' this book could be useful, and that generates an emotion which makes you 'feel' excited about reading it. Feelings manifest as physical sensations in your body, not as an idea in your mind. Perhaps, the reason the word 'feel' is so often overused or misused is because we don't want to talk about our emotions.

So, how do you feel now?

Why is it important to talk about emotions?

How you feel determines the quality of your life. Your emotions can make your life miserable or truly magical. That's why they are among the most essential things on which to focus. Your emotions color all your experiences. When you feel good, everything seems, feels, or tastes better. You also think better thoughts. Your energy levels are higher and possibilities seem limitless. Conversely, when you feel depressed, everything seems dull. You have little energy and you become unmotivated. You feel stuck in a place (mentally and physically) you don't want to be, and the future looks gloomy.

Your emotions can also act as a powerful guide. They can tell you something is wrong and allow you to make changes in your life. As such, they may be among the most powerful personal growth tools you have.

Sadly, neither your teachers nor your parents taught you how emotions work or how to control them. I find it ironic that just about anything comes with a how-to manual, while your mind doesn't. You've never received an instruction manual to teach you how your mind works and how to use it to better manage your emotions, have you? I haven't. In fact, until now, I doubt one even existed.

What you'll learn in this book

This book is the how-to manual your parents should have given you at birth. It's the instruction manual you should have received at school. In it, I'll share everything you need to know about emotions so you can overcome your fears and limitations and become the type of person you want to be.

More specifically, this book will help you:

- Understand what emotions are and how they impact your life
- Understand how emotions form and how you can use them for your personal growth
- Identify negative emotions that control your life and learn to overcome them
- Change your story to take better control over your life and create a more compelling future,
- Reprogram your mind to experience more positive emotions.
- Deal with negative emotions and condition your mind to create more positive ones

- Gain all the tools you need to start recognizing and controlling your emotions

Here is a more detailed summary of what you'll learn in this book:

In **Part I**, we'll discuss what emotions are. You'll learn why your brain is wired to focus on negativity and what you can do to counter this effect. You'll also discover how your beliefs impinge upon your emotions. Finally, you'll learn how negative emotions work and why they are so tricky.

In **Part II**, we'll go over the things that directly impact your emotions. You'll understand the roles your body, your thoughts, your words, or your sleep, play in your life and how you can use them to change your emotions.

In **Part III**, you'll learn how emotions form and how to condition your mind to experience more positive emotions.

And finally, in **Part IV**, we'll discuss how to use your emotions as a tool for personal growth. You'll learn why you experience emotions such as fear or depression and how they work.

Let's get started.

To start mastering your emotions today go to

mybook.to/Master_Emotions

I. What emotions are

Have you ever wondered what emotions are and what purpose they serve?

In this section, we'll discuss how your survival mechanism affects your emotions. Then, we'll explain what the 'ego' is and how it impacts your emotions. Finally, we'll discover the mechanism behind emotions and learn why it can be so hard to deal with negative ones.

Why people have a bias towards negativity

Your brain is designed for survival, which explains why you're able to read this book at this very moment. When you think about it, the probability of you being born was extremely low. For this miracle to happen, all the generations before you had to survive long enough to procreate. In their quest for survival and procreation, they must have faced death hundreds or perhaps thousands of times.

Fortunately, unlike your ancestors, you're (probably) not facing death every day. In fact, in many parts of the world, life has never been safer. Yet, your survival mechanism hasn't changed much. Your brain still scans your environment looking for potential threats.

In many ways, some parts of your brain have become obsolete. While you may not be seconds away from being eaten by a predator, your brain still gives significantly more weight to adverse events than to positive ones.

Fear of rejection is one example of a bias toward negativity. In the past, being rejected by your tribe would reduce your chances of survival significantly. Therefore, you learned to look for any sign of rejection, and this became hardwired in your brain.

Nowadays, being rejected often carries little or no consequence to your long-term survival. You can be hated by the entire world and still have a job, a roof and plenty of food on the table, yet, your brain remains programmed to perceive rejection as a threat to your survival.

This hardwiring is why rejection can be so painful. While you know most rejections are no big deal, you nevertheless feel the emotional pain. If you listen to your mind, you may even create a whole drama around it. You may believe you aren't worthy of love and dwell on a rejection for days or weeks. Worse still, you may become depressed as a result of this rejection.

One single criticism can often outweigh hundreds of positive ones. That's why, an author with fifty 5-star reviews, is likely to feel terrible when they receive a single 1-star review. While the author understands the 1-star review isn't a threat to her survival, her authorial brain doesn't. It likely interprets the negative review as a threat to her ego which triggers an emotional reaction.

The fear of rejection can also lead you to over-dramatize events. If your boss criticized you at work, your brain might see the criticism as a threat and you now think, "What if my boss fires me? What if I can't find a job quickly enough and my wife leaves me? What about my kids? What if I can't see them again?"

While you are fortunate to have such a useful survival mechanism, it is also your responsibility to separate real threats from imaginary ones. If you don't, you'll experience unnecessary pain and worry that will negatively impact the quality of your life. To overcome this bias towards negativity, you must reprogram your mind. One of a human being's greatest powers is our ability to use our thoughts to shape our reality and interpret events in a more empowering way. This book will teach you how to do this.

Why your brain's job isn't to make you happy

Your brain's primary responsibility is not to make you happy, but to ensure your survival. Thus, if you want to be happy, you must actively take control of your emotions rather than hoping you'll be happy because it's your natural state. In the following section, we'll discuss what happiness is and how it works.

How dopamine can mess with your happiness

Dopamine is a neurotransmitter that, among other functions, plays a significant role in rewarding certain behaviors. When dopamine releases into specific areas of your brain—the pleasure centers—you get an intense sense of wellbeing similar to a high. This sense of wellbeing is what happens during exercise, when you gamble, have sex, or eat great food.

One of the roles of dopamine is to ensure you look for food so you don't die of starvation, and you search for a mate so you can reproduce. Without dopamine, our species would likely be extinct by now. It's a pretty good thing, right?

Well, yes and no. In today's world, this reward system is, in many cases, obsolete. In the past, dopamine directly linked to our survival, now, it can be stimulated artificially. A great example of this effect is social media, which uses psychology to suck as much time as possible out of your life. Have you noticed all these notifications that pop up regularly? They're used to trigger a release of dopamine so you stay connected, and the longer you stay connected, the more money the services make. Watching pornography or gambling also leads to a release of dopamine which can make these activities highly addictive.

Fortunately, we don't need to act each time our brain releases dopamine. For instance, we don't need to continuously check our Facebook newsfeeds just because it gives us a pleasurable shot of dopamine.

Today's society is selling a version of happiness that can make us *un*happy. We've become addicted to dopamine mainly because of marketers who have found effective ways to exploit our brains. We receive multiple shots of dopamine throughout the day and we love it. But is that the same thing as happiness?

Worse than that, dopamine can create real addictions with severe consequences on our health. Research conducted at Tulane University showed that, when permitted to self-stimulate their pleasure center, participants did it an average of forty times per minute. They chose the stimulation of their pleasure center over food, even refusing to eat when hungry!

Korean, Lee Seung Seop is an extreme case of this syndrome. In 2005, Mr Seop died after playing a video game for fifty-eight hours straight with very little food or water, and no sleep. The subsequent investigation concluded the cause of death was heart failure induced by exhaustion and dehydration. He was only twenty-eight years old.

To take control of your emotions, you must understand the role dopamine plays and how it affects your happiness. Are you addicted to your phone? Are you glued to your TV? Or maybe you spend too much time playing video games. Most of us are addicted to something. For some people it's obvious, but for others, it's more subtle. For instance, you could be addicted to thinking. To better control your emotions, you must recognize and shed the light on your addictions as they can rob you of your happiness.

The 'one day I will' myth

Do you believe that one day you will achieve your dream and finally be happy? It is unlikely to happen. You may (and I hope you will) achieve your goal, but you won't live 'happily ever after.' This thinking is just another trick your mind plays on you.

Your mind quickly acclimates to new situations, which is probably the result of evolution and our need to adapt continually to survive and reproduce. This acclimatization is also probably why the new car or house you want will only make you happy for a while. Once the initial excitement wears off, you'll move on to crave the next exciting thing. This phenomenon is known as 'hedonic adaptation.'

How hedonic adaptation works

Let me share an interesting study that will likely change the way you see happiness. This study, which was conducted in 1978 on lottery winners and paraplegics, was incredibly eye-opening for me. The investigation evaluated how winning the lottery or becoming a paraplegic influence happiness:

The study found that one year after the event, both groups were just as happy as they were beforehand. Yes, just as happy (or unhappy). You can find more about it by watching Dan Gilbert's TED Talk, The Surprising Science of Happiness.

Perhaps you believe that you'll be happy once you've 'made it.' But, as the above study on happiness shows, this is simply not true. No matter what happens to you, your mind works by reverting to your predetermined level of happiness once you've adapted to the new event.

Does that mean you can't be happier than you are right now? No.

What it means is that, in the long run, external events have minimal impact on your level of happiness.

In fact, according to Sonja Lyubomirsky, author of *The How of Happiness*, fifty percent of our happiness is determined by genetics, forty percent by internal factors, and only ten percent by external factors. These external factors include such things as whether we're single or married, rich or poor, and similar social influences.

The influence of external factors is probably way less than you thought. The bottom line is this: Your attitude towards life influences your happiness, not what happens to you.

By now, you understand how your survival mechanism negatively impacts your emotions and prevents you from experiencing more joy and happiness in your life. In the next section, we'll learn about the ego.

To read more visit my author page at:

amazon.com/author/thibautmeurisse

OTHER BOOKS BY THE AUTHORS:

Crush Your Limits: Break Free from Limitations and Achieve Your True Potential

Goal Setting: The Ultimate Guide to Achieving Life-Changing Goals

Habits That Stick: The Ultimate Guide to Building Habits That Stick Once and For All

Master Your Destiny: A Practical Guide to Rewrite Your Story and Become the Person You Want to Be

Master Your Emotions: A Practical Guide to Overcome Negativity and Better Manage Your Feelings

Master Your Focus: A Practical Guide to Stop Chasing the Next Thing and Focus on What Matters Until It's Done

Master Your Motivation: A Practical Guide to Unstick Yourself, Build Momentum and Sustain Long-Term Motivation

Master Your Thinking: A Practical Guide to Align Yourself with Reality and Achieve Tangible Results in the Real World

Productivity Beast: An Unconventional Guide to Getting Things Done

The Greatness Manifesto: Overcome Your Fear and Go After What You Really Want

The One Goal: Master the Art of Goal Setting, Win Your Inner Battles, and Achieve Exceptional Results

The Passion Manifesto: Escape the Rat Race, Uncover Your Passion and Design a Career and Life You Love

The Thriving Introvert: Embrace the Gift of Introversion and Live the Life You Were Meant to Live

The Ultimate Goal Setting Planner: Become an Unstoppable Goal Achiever in 90 Days or Less

Upgrade Yourself: Simple Strategies to Transform Your Mindset, Improve Your Habits and Change Your Life

Success is Inevitable: 17 Laws to Unlock Your Hidden Potential, Skyrocket

Your Confidence and Get What You Want From Life

Wake Up Call: How To Take Control Of Your Morning And Transform Your Life

ABOUT THE AUTHOR

THIBAUT MEURISSE

Thibaut Meurisse is a personal development blogger, author, and founder of whatispersonaldevelopment.org. M

Obsessed with self-improvement and fascinated by the power of the brain, his personal mission is to help people realize their full potential and reach higher levels of fulfillment and consciousness.

In love with foreign languages, he is French, writes in English, and lived in Japan for almost ten years.

Learn more about Thibaut at:

amazon.com/author/thibautmeurisse
whatispersonaldevelopment.org
thibaut.meurisse@gmail.com

ACTION GUIDE

Section I. Taking responsibility

1. Start where you are

Take a moment to acknowledge that you are exactly where you're supposed to be *at this moment* and let go of any sense of pressure.

Get excited about all the things you can do to improve and start moving toward your dreams. Write some of them using the space below.

2. Take one hundred percent responsibility for your life

Write down two or three things you would do differently if you were to take one hundred percent responsibility for everything in your life:

-

-

-

3. Take extra responsibility

Complete the exercise below

Write down one thing that currently bothers you:

Write down what you think the root cause might be:

Write down what you could have done differently to prevent the issue from happening in the first place:

4. Forget about luck

If luck didn't exist, what would I do to maximize my chances of achieving my biggest goal?

5. Value your time above all

What exactly does "valuing your time" mean to me?

What are two specific things I could do to make better use of my time?

1.

2.

6. Follow your own path

If I were to follow my own path, what would I be doing?

If I didn't have to worry about what my family, friends, colleagues or society think, what would I be doing?

7. Embrace your destiny

What is my true calling? What's my intuition telling me?

What fears do I need to overcome to move in the right direction?

8. Forgive yourself and others

Take a couple of minutes to:

- Acknowledge that your peace of mind is more important than anything anyone may have done to you in the past. Stop trying to be right, try to be happy.
- Forgive yourself for mistakes you may have made in the past. You did what you could based on what you knew and who you were at the time. You can write down below what you want to forgive yourself.

Section II. Knowing yourself

9. Cultivate self-awareness

If I were to be more self-aware, what specific thing would have the biggest positive impact on my life?

What is the one negative emotion I experience most often?

What is the underlying belief causing me to feel this way?

10. Define what success means to you

Write down five must-haves for a successful life.

1.

2.

3.

4.

5.

Based on these must-haves, come up with your own personal definition of success and summarize it in one or two sentences below.

My personal definition of success:

11. Know what you want

Spend five to ten minutes brainstorming answers to the question, "What do I really want?" Do this for each area of your life: career, finance, health, personal growth relationships and spirituality.

Career:

Finance:

Health:

Personal growth:

Relationships:

Spirituality:

12. Know what matters to you

Write down your top 10 values below. If you're unsure what a value is, simply ask yourself what thing or concept you value the most (freedom, family, contribution, honesty et cetera).

1.

2.

3.

4.

5.

6.

7.

8.

9.

10.

Select your top three values by asking yourself, "If I could choose only one value, what would it be?" Repeat the process until you have your three values. Then on a scale of 1 to 10, where 1 is low and 10 is high, ask yourself how well you're living by these values.

Value #1:

How well you're currently living by it

0   10

Value #2:

How well you're currently living by it

0   10

Value #3:

How well you're currently living by it

0	10

Finally, answer the following question:

Which is the one specific thing I could start doing today that will be more aligned with one or more of these values?

13. Know your strength

Identify your biggest strengths by answer the questions below:

What people around you say your strengths? Ask at least one person who knows you well and write down your answers below:

What do you do during your spare time? Write down anything you do spontaneously when you have free time:

What can you do easily (but others can't)?

What people compliment you for?

What do you really enjoy doing?

14. Embrace your weaknesses

Write down below what you believe to be your biggest weaknesses.

Then ask yourself:

What would happen if I took these weaknesses to extremes? How could I turn some of them into strengths?

Who or what can help me overcome these weaknesses?

15. Listen to your intuition

What single thing could you do to listen to your intuition better?

Section III. Deciding who you want to be

16. Decide who you're going to be

Look at one of your major goals. What would happen if you were absolutely committed to achieving it? What would you do if attaining this goal was a matter of life or death? Write down your answer below:

17. Be intentional during your day

What would it mean to me to have more "intent" during my day? What specific things would I do?

18. Raise your standards

If you chose to do one single thing to help you raise your standards significantly, what would it be?

19. Cultivate self-discipline

To build self-discipline, choose one positive habit that would improve your life and resolve to stick to it for the next thirty days. Make sure you start small to avoid putting too much pressure on yourself.

My positive habit:

20. Build accountability

How could you build an accountability system that works for you?

Write down what your ideal accountability system would look like.

21. Create a morning ritual

Create your own morning ritual including 2-3 simple daily habits. Then, commit to sticking to it for at least the next thirty days.

My 2-3 simps daily habits:

-

-

-

22. Find people worth fighting for

Who do I want to fight for?

Who do I feel a strong desire to serve?

Section IV. Living with integrity

23. Respect yourself

What are three specific things you could do to show yourself more respect? Write them down below:

1.

2.

3.

24. Practice radical honesty with yourself

Is my current life really what I want?

What questions am I avoiding asking myself, and why?

Knowing what I now know, if I could start all over, what would I do differently? What actions could I take now?

If my future self—now five years older—were to talk to me, what would he/she tell me?

Am I really doing whatever it takes to achieve the goals I say I want to achieve?

25. Practice radical honesty with others

Who are you not sharing your honest feelings with?

By failing to give people the honest feedback they deserve, who are you preventing from improving?

26. Learn to say no

If you could say "no" to anything without experiencing shame, guilt or any other negative feelings, exactly what would you say no to? Write them all down below.

-

-

-

-

-

-

-

-

-

-

27. Set clear rules and boundaries

Complete the following exercise:

1. Write down the things you tolerate in your life, but you wish were different.

2. Establish clear rules you can stand behind. Write them down below (be specific).

3. Imagine yourself acting according to your defined boundaries when the situation presents itself. To do so, rehearse your responses in your mind, using visualization.

4. Remind yourself that you have the right to set your own rules and boundaries and that not everyone will be happy about it.

28. Show up on time

Strive to arrive on time (or earlier) to every business meeting in the next thirty days until it becomes a habit.

29. Take pride in your work

Answer the following questions:

Am I doing the best I can at work/school?

If I were to step into my best self, what would I do differently?

How can I become more engaged at work? What can I deep dive into instead of running away from? Who can I interact with more often and at a deeper level?

30. Cultivate a passion for what you do

When do I feel the most engaged at work? What specifically am I doing in these moments?

What do I volunteer for at work or outside of work? How can I do more of these things?

Additional step: choose one activity you enjoy and dedicate 10-15 minutes to pursuing it every day.

31. Ask for what you want

This week, ask for one thing you want, whether it be small or big. For instance, you could ask for a discount, a small favor or an upgrade.

What I will ask or this week:

32. Be a producer, not a consumer

Answer the following questions:

If I shifted from being a consumer to a producer, what would it mean to me? What would I be doing differently? What would I create?

What can I do to better express my unique personality and creativity?

Write down one unproductive activity you regularly engage in. Then, write down one productive activity you could engage in instead.

Unproductive activity:

Productivity activity you could engage in instead:

Section V. Cultivating confidence

33. Believe you can

Select one of your biggest goals or dreams and allow yourself to believe you can achieve it.

My biggest goals:

All the reasons I believe I can achieve it:

-

-

-

-

-

All the things I could do to start moving toward that goal:

-

-

-

-

-

Imagine you have already achieved this goal. Then, relax and allow yourself to feel good about it.

34. Believe that who you are and what you do matters

- Close your eyes. Then, allow yourself to let go of any need for approval (from your parents, friends, colleagues, society et cetera). Imagine how freeing it will be if you don't need to prove anything to anyone.
- Appreciate yourself just for existing and acknowledge your inherent value as an individual human being with a unique personality.
- Think of all the people you've ever helped in even the smallest way.
- Feel good for being you.

35. Challenge your limiting beliefs

Select one area of your life and ask yourself why you're not at a 10/10 in this area:

Write down all the reasons (or excuses) you came up with:

-

-

-

-

-

Challenge them. Are they really true? Write down any counter argument you can think of:

Find specific examples that disprove each of these reasons or beliefs (whether in your personal life or in other people's lives) and write them down:

Choose the empowering belief you want to adopt instead.

Create an affirmation using the tips below:

- Use present tense,
- Use the first person, and
- Make it specific and keep it short.

For instance, if you believe you don't have enough time, you could use the affirmation below:

"I always make the time to do whatever I'm committed to."

My affirmation:

36. Focus on what you want

Write down one thing you want:

Find at least one group of people moving toward the same goal, either online or offline. Write it down below:

For the next seven days:

- Write three things you are grateful for related to that thing.
- Spend a few minutes every day reading books and articles on the topic.
- Take one small action to move closer to your goal.

37. Cultivate optimism

What are two or three specific things you could do to cultivate a greater sense of optimism?

-

-

-

38. Perceive the opportunities around you

1. Answer the following questions:

What can be improved around me?

What do I need to learn, in order for new opportunities to open up for me?

What opportunities are so obvious that I may have missed them?

2. Ask someone close to you what opportunities they see for you.

3. Practice write down ten new ideas each morning on any topic of interest and start perceiving more opportunities around you.

39. Think big

1. Envision the craziest and most unrealistic dream you can think of.
2. Think of the smallest action you could take to move closer to those dreams.
3. Take that small action today and see where it takes you.

40. Believe you will improve long-term

1. Look at one of the things you can do well.
2. Remember a time where you couldn't do that thing.
3. Think of something you want to become great at.
4. Assume mastering that thing is inevitable in the mid to long term.

41. Celebrate your success

At the end of your day, ask yourself:

"What are the three things I'm most proud of having done today?"

42. Move beyond your comfort zone

What does "moving beyond your comfort zone" mean to you?

Remember one time you pushed beyond your comfort zone. How did it make you feel?

Think of one uncomfortable thing you could do today or later this week and decide to undertake it.

The one uncomfortable thing I could do:

43. Practice positive self-talk

For 24 hours, observe your self-talk. How is the little voice inside you treating you? Notice when you criticize yourself and what impacts it has on your mental well-being.

44. Practice visualization

Take a couple of minutes now to visualize yourself in a specific situation. It can be a future goal you want to achieve or an uncomfortable situation you want to handle better. See yourself feeling, thinking and acting the way you want to.

Section VI. Developing an accurate model of reality

45. Understand that success is a process

Write down one meaningful goal you want to achieve:

Identify the best process to help you reach that goal. What daily habits could you implement? What key tasks would you focus on?

46. Align yourself with reality

Reflect on the two questions below in relation to your previous goal:

In what ways am I trying to fight against reality?

How does it make me feel?

47. See failures as part of the process

In which areas of your life are you not trying and failing enough?

If you weren't afraid of failure, what would you do differently in those areas?

48. Look for role models

Identify one or two people who have already achieved the meaningful goal you're chasing. Then, resolve to learn everything you can from them.

My role model(s):

49. Dramatically reduce your learning curve

Answer the following questions about your goal:

How can I reach it as quickly and with as little effort as possible?

Who has the best blueprint for this specific goal?

If I were to perform certain key tasks every day, consistently, which ones are most likely to guarantee my success?

50. Focus on solutions

Write down three to five things you're currently worrying about.

-

-

-

-

-

Now write down what you can do about each of them.

51. Don't assume, verify

What are the biggest assumptions you might be making in your life right now? Write down a few of them.

What are the consequences of holding onto these assumptions?

52. Cultivate long-term thinking

Where do you want to be mentally, physically and financially ten years from now? And why is that important to you?

53. Schedule thinking time

Schedule one hour of thinking time either today or later this week. Check whether you're moving in the right direction and brainstorm innovative ways to improve your life or to reach your goals.

When I'll do my hour of thinking time:

54. Challenge the status quo

What is one thing that most people accept but you're unwilling to do the same?

What are you going to do about it?

55. Ask smart questions

Write three of the most empowering questions you can think of. Start reflecting on them and do so for at least a few minutes.

The three most empowering questions I can think of:

1.

2.

3.

56. Take calculated risks

What risk do you feel like taking in the near future?

What can you do to ensure it's a calculated risk with limited downsides but huge upsides?

57. Better anticipate

Write down one issue you're facing right now.

Now go back to its root cause and ask yourself, "What could I have done to avoid that problem and/or limit its negative impact on my life?"

Section VII. Getting things done

58. Set daily goals

- Identify three to five tasks that you will work on today (make sure they move you closer to your long-term vision).
- Complete the first task before moving on to other tasks.
- Repeat this process until you complete all your tasks.

Bonus tip: an effective way to ensure you work on your most valuable task every day is to make it part of your morning ritual (see also *Chapter 21. Create a morning ritual*).

59. Finish what you start

Do one of the two things below:

1 .Write down three simple tasks and complete them today. Repeat this process for seven days:

-

-

-

2. Complete a task you've been procrastinating on for a while and complete it one hundred percent.

60. Think less, do more

Write down one thing you've been procrastinating on due to fear:

Then, take that first step you've been avoiding for far too long.

61. Leverage The 80/20 Principle

Select one area of your life and write it down below:

Now create an exhaustive list of all the actions you're currently taking.

Finally, answer the question below:

Of these actions, which 20% lead to 80% of your results in this specific area?

Circle one to three key actions that you believe are the most effective. These are the tasks you want to focus on. A good idea is to make them part of your morning ritual (See *Chapter 21. Create a morning ritual*).

62. Maximize your speed of implementation

Select one exciting goal and write it down below:

Imagine you were given a power called, "Extreme speed of implementation". What can you do right now to make progress toward that goal?

63. Get started

Write down your first step. This first step could be toward the achievement of any sort of goals in any area of your life. That's up to you.

My first step:

Take that first step today or later this week and see where it takes you.

64. Focus on the process

Write down one goal you want to achieve (a result goal).

Now write down the process goals that will most likely lead you to achieve that goal:

65. Think projects not tasks

Reflect on the tasks you've been working on in the past seven days. Now, think of the few key projects you are trying to complete. Are these the most important tasks you should be focusing on to complete these projects? If not, what could you be doing differently?

66. Focus on one thing at a time

Make a list of all the major projects you're currently working on using the space below:

-

-

-

-

If I could only focus on one thing, what would that thing be?

Now how will you allocate time during the day to focus single-mindedly on it? (I recommend you make it part of your morning ritual whenever possible).

67. Eliminate distractions and boost your focus

Today, practice working on one task for forty-five minutes without interruption. Whenever you catch your mind wandering, bring your attention to the task at hand.

68. Go temporarily out of balance

If you decided to focus most of your time and effort on one area right now, which one would have the biggest positive impact on your life?

69. Be a master, not a dabbler

Think of one goal you failed to achieve in the past.

Now, imagine how things would have been different if you had a mastery mindset.

Write down below a few things you would have done differently:

Then, select one of your major goals and imagine what working on it with a mastery mindset would look like.

70. Fall in love with consistency

Select one daily habit and write it down below:

Then, commit to sticking to it for the next thirty days in a row.

71. Take effective breaks

Experiment with each of the time-blocks below for a week. Then, select the one that works best for you.

- **Every seventy-five to ninety minutes:** Robert Pozen, author of *Extreme Productivity: Boost Your Results, Reduce Your Hours*, recommends taking a break every seventy-five to ninety minutes.
- **Every fifty-two minutes:** The startup, Draugiem Group, found that the most productive people took frequent breaks, working fifty-two minutes and taking seventeen-minute rests.
- **Every twenty-five minutes (Pomodoro technique):** The Pomodoro technique entails working twenty-five minutes and taking five-minute breaks.

Section VIII. Maintaining an open mind

72. Leverage your curiosity

What is the one thing you're the most curious about?

Go learn more about that thing by reading articles online, buying a book or taking a course.

73. Embrace flexibility

Select a major goal you're working on right now and write it down below:

Do you enjoy working on this goal?

Does it help you design the future I want?

If not, what could you do about it? Could you revise your goal? Could you just give up on it and focus on another goal?

74. Never stop learning

Develop the habit of reading or listening to educational content for fifteen minutes every day.

75. Stay humble

In what ways are you not as humble as you could be? Write down some of your answers. below:

What one specific thing could you do to change that?

76. Make the most of your mistakes

What failures are you refusing to face head-on and learn from?

What mistakes may you be making right now or in the near future?

What could you do about it?

77. Let go of your ego

How is pride preventing you from living the life you want?

Section IX. Developing emotional resilience

78. Embrace patience

Remind yourself to be patient and refer the book as often as necessary until you have a solid grasp of the principles introduced in it.

79. Treat each day as a new beginning

For the next few days, experiment with the process below (smile, act, acknowledge, clear, express gratitude and plan). See how it makes you feel.

- **Smile.** As soon as you wake up, smile. This simple act will boost your mood over time.
- **Act.** Don't hit the snooze button. Jump out of bed immediately. This will help build the habit of being proactive and decisive.
- **Acknowledge.** Think how lucky you are to have been granted a new day. This is the first step to making your day count.
- **Clear.** Start your day as a blank canvas. To do so, visualize yourself letting go of the burden of your past. For instance, picture your past as a ball and chain. Break free from your chains and feel yourself becoming lighter and lighter. This will help you be more present during the day.
- **Express gratitude.** Think of three things you're grateful for or do one of the exercises introduced in *Chapter 85. Cultivate gratitude.* This will boost your mood and reduce your negative emotions.
- **Plan.** Write down today's date as well as your goals for the day. This will help you give more importance to your day while boosting your productivity.

80. Focus on what you can control

Using the table below, take a few minutes to write a few things you're worrying about. Then, in the right-hand column, write down whether you have total control (TC) some control (SC) or no control (NC) over the situation.

Things you worry about	TC, SC or NC?

81. Leverage the power of reframing

Think of one negative event that happened to you recently and write it down below:

What was great about it?

What valuable lesson did/could you learn from it?

How did you turn (or how could you have turned) this situation into an opportunity?

82. Honor the struggle

Remember the difficult times you had to go through to reach your current position. In hindsight, what would you say to your past self? Then, say the same thing to your present self and see how it feels.

83. Cultivate self-compassion

For the next seven days, speak to yourself only in a gentle, supportive way. Whenever you're harsh with yourself notice it and refocus on being kind to yourself.

84. Prepare for the worst

Think of one major goal you're currently working toward.

Now write down some of the worst-case scenarios you can think of:

-

-

-

-

Imagine yourself going through each of them. What would be your initial reaction?

Finally, see yourself pushing through these obstacles.

85. Practice gratitude

Think of ten things you're the most grateful for right now.

Adopt a daily gratitude practice using one of the exercises introduced below

- **Write down what you're grateful for.** Write down three things you're grateful for and try to come up with three different things every day.
- **Create a gratitude journal.** Buy a notebook and use it to record any compliments you receive. Keep adding new entries, and go through old ones every day, or at least a few times a week.
- **Thank people.** Close your eyes and think of the first person that comes to mind. Then, thank that person (in your mind). Try to thank them for at least one specific thing they did for you. Perhaps they helped you find a job. Perhaps they were there for you during challenging times. Perhaps they taught you a lesson. Repeat the process with a second person. Keep doing this for three to five minutes. To help you experience feelings of gratitude, you can listen to a song that moves you while doing this exercise.

86. Learn from your emotions

Think of one negative emotion you experienced recently and write it down below:

What can you learn from that particular emotion? What is it trying to tell you?

87. Exercise regularly

Write down a simple exercise routine you could see yourself following for months or years. Remember that being consistent is key. Start small. You can always intensify your workout over time.

My simple exercise routine:

Section X. Influencing and inspiring others

88. Share your dreams/broadcast your desires

What goal could you broadcast to the world and how will you do it?

89. See yourself as a role model

Who has changed for the better as a result of spending time around you?

What could you do specifically to become an even better source of inspiration to the people around me?

90. Aim to change yourself before changing others

If you were to change something within yourself, what specific thing would allow you to have the biggest possible impact on the world around you?

91. Add value to other people's lives

How can you deliver more value to the people around you?

92. Believe in the potential of others

Close your eyes and visualize the people close to you (family members, friends, colleagues, et cetera). For each person you visualize, imagine them as having achieved their absolute potential. Envision how they would feel, think and act. See all the wonderful things they would be accomplishing.

93. Be obsessed with your customers

How can you give your customers what they truly want?

94. Compliment others

Think of five people you spend a lot of time with and give one genuine compliment to each of them (in your mind).

Try to think of something you've never told them before. Then, challenge yourself to give them that compliment in real life.

95. Seek a win-win

Think of someone with whom you are having a disagreement and write his or her name below:

What could you do to create a win-win relationship with that person?

96. Ask more questions, give fewer answers

Today, notice whenever you feel like giving an answer or offering advice. Then, pause and ask yourself what question you could ask instead.

97. Listen more, talk less

Practice active listening during one of your conversations today. Don't listen to take control of the conversation or give advice. Don't think what you're going to say next. Just listen without judging.

98. Put yourself in the shoes of other people

Select three people close to you and try to define their values and goals.

Person #1:

Values:

Goals:

Person #2:

Values:

Goals:

Person #3:

Values:

Goals:

Then, go ask them directly. For instance, share your values first and ask them what their values are. Ask them where they see themselves in ten years.

99. Surround yourself with successful people

Who is one negative person you want to spend less time with?

Who is one friend or acquaintance that, if you were to spend more time with, would allow you to grow and learn faster?

If you could connect with one person to have the most positive impact in the long term, who would it be?

100. Focus on building long-term relationships

Who do you want to connect with?

Specifically, what could you do to help that person?